Praise for *The Gift of Dyslexia:*

"What do Cher, Leonardo da Vinci, Whoopi Goldberg, and Walt Disney all have in common? Dyslexia. Though one may think they achieved success *in spite* of their disability, Ronald D. Davis, author of *The Gift of Dyslexia*, says it's *because* of it . . . Davis's procedure enjoys a 97 percent success rate. Once students remove obstacles to learning, they are free to capitalize on the innate gifts dyslexia can bring."
—*New Woman*

"A unique perspective on the subject of learning disabilities. Through his own real-life experiences he shares what everyone needs to know about dyslexia . . ."
—*Library Journal*

". . . now a new teaching method—in which dyslexics model key words in clay—promises to put an end to the problems of dyslexia once and for all."
—*The Independent* (England)

". . . expresses understanding and encouragement for all those lost in a world of confusion and frustration."
—*Eclectic Book Reviews*

"Davis stands the concept of dyslexia on its head."
—*The Jerusalem Post*

THE GIFT
OF LEARNING

Proven New Methods for Correcting
ADD, Math & Handwriting Problems

Ronald D. Davis with Eldon M. Braun

A PERIGEE BOOK

Davis Dyslexia Correction®, Davis Orientation Counseling®, Davis Math Mastery®, Davis Symbol Mastery®, Davis ADD Mastery™, Davis Learning Strategies®, the DDAI logo and the name Davis™ are trademarks of Ronald D. Davis and Davis Dyslexia Association International.

Illustrations on pp. 42, 54, 177, 231, 303, 324, and 330 by Kevin Wood.

"One Man Band" illustration on p. 237 from an original sculpture by Mark Steele, courtesy Intellution Software.

Material on p. 63 reprinted from *Mark Twain: A Biography*, by Albert Bigelow Paine, Chelsea House Publishers, 1997. Used by permission.

A Perigee Book
Published by The Berkley Publishing Group
A division of Penguin Group (USA) Inc.
375 Hudson Street
New York, New York 10014

First edition: August 2003

Library of Congress Cataloging-in-Publication Data

Davis, Ronald D. (Ronald Dell), 1942–
    The gift of learning : proven new methods for correcting ADD, math & handwriting problems / Ronald D. Davis with Eldon M. Braun.
        p. cm.
    Includes bibliographical references and index.
    ISBN 0-399-52809-1
    1. Learning disabled—Education—Handbooks, manuals, etc.   I. Braun, Eldon M., 1943–
II. Title.

LC4704 .D38   2002
371.92'6—dc21

2002025123

Printed in the United States of America

10   9   8   7   6   5   4   3   2   1

In honor and memory of
Harold Joseph Anderson,
one man who cared

CONTENTS

SECTION THREE
Addressing ADD and ADHD

SECTION FOUR
Addressing Math

SECTION FIVE
Addressing Handwriting

by Thom Hartmann

I was only seven years old, but can still remember my second grade teacher, Mrs. Clark. She was a large, motherly, caring woman with a thick southern drawl and a dedication to teaching I still hold in awe. I was one of her most hyperactive students, and can still hear her voice saying to me, "Tommy, an empty wagon always rattles!" and, "Even a fish wouldn't get caught if it kept its mouth shut!" And I remember to this day the feeling of disorientation I experienced when she'd get angry with me.

But it wasn't until I read this book by Ron Davis that I understood what that disorientation meant or why I was experiencing it. Ron Davis is a revolutionary and profound thinker, and has discovered what history will record as one of the great insights in the fields of learning and how the mind works. This is seminal work, a profound insight into a very real problem.

Another validation for me of Ron's work, in retrospect, was my discovery when I was sixteen of the works of Gurdjieff and Ouspensky. I read Ouspensky's

In Search of the Miraculous and *The Fourth Way*, and began then to practice a technique Ouspensky learned from Gurdjieff back in the late nineteenth century: Create an "observer" just behind and above the back of your head and, from that point of observation, watch everything going on in your own head while watching at the same time, through your head and eyes in front of you, the world around you. Gurdjieff's technique (this is only one facet of it) reflects others variously known as Vipassana, mindfulness, and an NLP technique having to do with orientation and submodality shifts. Gurdjieff claimed it would bring about enlightenment and perhaps even psychic powers.

As a teenager, the technique I learned by reading Ouspensky's book grounded me powerfully. I've been using it and variations of it pretty continuously for the nearly forty years since then. And now Ron brings the world a new, easier, and more rapid version of something somewhat similar to it as a tool to resolve learning disabilities. Brilliant!

Most likely, at this point in reading this foreword, you're experiencing a bit of disorientation of your own, as I haven't well explained the concepts I'm discussing. That's good—it means your mind is telling you you've encountered something new, are ready to learn, and that you've had a small sample of the daily fare for some children with learning disabilities.

And, because Ron does such a brilliant job of explaining his concepts and remedies, I'll keep this foreword short and suggest you now begin reading the following text, which will forever transform your understanding of how some children and adults experience the world.

—Thom Hartmann
Montpelier, Vermont

Thom Hartmann, writer, entrepreneur, psychotherapist, and worldwide lecturer, is the creator of the "Hunter in a Farmer's World" metaphor for describing ADD and ADHD, and the author of eight books on Attention Deficit Disorder. Each of his books contains information on education, psychology, psychotherapy, and how to reinvent our schools, workplaces and other aspects of our culture to work for all children and adults, including those with ADD or other learning disabilities.

INTRODUCTION

When I was eighteen years old, I was unable to read, write, or spell, despite having an IQ of 137. For years I had struggled in school to master the basics of reading and writing, but to no avail. I could solve math problems in my head and produce the answers, but I couldn't show how I got them. I went to a doctor who told me I would never be able to master the alphabet and learn to read. He believed that my brain had been damaged at birth. I accepted his diagnosis because I believed doctors knew everything there was to know about such things, and I didn't know any better.

As a result of this doctor's diagnosis, I spent the next twenty years coping with a severe learning disability. I didn't read books or newspapers, and I couldn't sit still long enough to watch much television. What the average person could read in five minutes or less would take me an hour or more. I could mentally compose a single-paragraph letter in seconds, but it might take four to five hours to get it down on paper. So it wasn't that I was entirely incapable of doing these things. They were simply so difficult and time-consuming that I didn't do them. By 1980, I was thirty-eight years old and still functionally illiterate.

However, I did manage to complete my education and become a certified mechanical engineer. Because of this training and background, I kept trying to find a logical solution to my reading and handwriting problems. The medical establishment certainly was of little help. But through a series of self-administered experiments, I discovered a rudimentary form of what I now call "orientation." I learned to stabilize my perceptions so that the words fell into place. I discovered that while in this "oriented state," I was able to read without any of the problems I had encountered before. But as excited as I was by this success, I soon realized that all I had done was discover one piece of a much larger puzzle.

In July of 1981, I founded the Reading Research Council with Dr. Fatima Ali, an educational psychologist. Our goal was to find the other pieces of the puzzle, then try to put them all together in order to actually correct the learning difficulties associated with dyslexia.

By April of 1982, we had developed a method known as the Davis Orientation Counseling Procedure that could correct the problems of dyslexia. We opened the Davis Dyslexia Correction Center to offer our services to the general public and began treating dyslexics of all ages.

At this point, you might be wondering just what all of this has to do with attention deficit disorder (ADD) and math and handwriting learning disabilities. Most people think dyslexia is only a reading problem, because this is the common understanding of the disability. But soon after we opened our doors to the public, we began to see many dyslexics, both children and adults, who also had problems with math, handwriting, and who exhibited many of the symptoms of ADD, such as staying focused or sitting still. Some students displayed problems with just one or two areas, some had problems with all three, some just with reading. I had problems myself with reading and handwriting, and exhibited some of the symptoms of ADD. At first we considered these other disabilities to be separate and not related, until we discovered that applying the basic principles of orientation seemed to help correct some of them. This led us to conclude that perhaps there was a connection after all.

For more than twenty years, we have continued to develop and refine the original Davis Orientation Counseling Procedure, expanding it to include exercises to help treat these other disabilities. We have treated thousands of clients with an overall success rate higher than 90 percent.

As our reputation grew, so did the demand for our services. We published our first book *The Gift of Dyslexia,* in 1994, which contains the Davis Orientation Procedure and additional exercises to treat dyslexia. We then established the Davis Dyslexia Association International (DDAI) in 1995 to train "facilitators" to administer the Davis Dyslexia Correction, Davis Math Mastery, and Davis ADD Mastery programs. The training program consists of approximately four hundred hours of workshops, field assignments, supervised practice meetings, and training pods. After completion of this program, Davis Facilitators are fully prepared to address most of the learning disability symptoms and characteristics they are likely to encounter.

As of this writing, facilitator training is provided in six different languages around the world. Last year, more than ten thousand learning-disabled children and adults successfully eliminated their symptoms of dyslexia, ADD, and handwriting and math problems.

So the real purpose of this book isn't just to give you an alternative theory behind these various learning disabilities; it is to provide you with a method to treat them. However, understanding the true nature of a problem is a prerequisite to finding a real solution. If any problem isn't fully understood, attempts to solve it won't be very effective. So first I want to share my understanding and knowledge of these problems, and then I will share the process for correcting them. My intention is that you will be able to use this book to help someone eliminate his or her particular learning problems by guiding them through a correction process, step by step.

The first section of this book offers the foundation of our theory on orientation, disorientation, and picture thinking, and their relationship to ADD, math, and handwriting. The second section offers our "Basic Tool Package," techniques based on our original orientation procedure. Most or all of them need to be performed first before moving on to the specific exercises for

ADD, math, and handwriting disabilities. Although I realize many of you will be tempted to skip ahead to the specific exercises, I urge you to read the first section on theory before proceeding to the instructional section of this book.

If you are a concerned parent of a child that has been diagnosed as "learning disabled," or perhaps a concerned teacher who wishes to help a student, you have purchased this book because you have refused to accept that the child is incapable of overcoming his or her disabilities. The questions you should ask yourself before proceeding are:

What is your understanding of the child's problem?

Where did you get that information about the child?

What is being done to correct the problem?

Is the child making any progress?

Is the child failing in the system, or is the system failing the child?

Do you really believe that more of the same methods that have failed so far are ever going to work?

Are you open to exploring new ideas and solutions?

More than twenty years ago, a life experience brought me to a point where I had to question the validity of my beliefs about my own learning disability.

I discovered that I wasn't "brain damaged," and went on to develop solutions—first for myself, and then for others like me. Those solutions are the true purpose of this book.

SECTION ONE

The Learning Process and Disabilities

CHAPTER 1

Defining Learning and Learning Disability

The word "learning" itself has a wide range of meanings for people, and a vast selection of references are available to define it. I simply looked up the word in my favorite dictionary, *The New Lexicon Webster's.* This is how it defines the word *learn*:

> learn: *v.t.* to acquire knowledge of or skill in by study, instruction, practice, or experience—to commit to memory—to come to know or be aware of.

Obviously, this definition describes different levels or degrees of learning.

Knowledge of a subject doesn't necessarily mean you can do anything with it. That would require *skill.* Likewise, a student can commit something to memory with no knowledge whatsoever. A grade-schooler, for example, might be able to recite the multiplication table perfectly, but still be unable to solve simple math problems. *Coming to know* something implies the goal of being able to use the knowledge, while *being aware of* facts or figures does not.

Of the methods for acquiring knowledge, *study* and *instruction* are the two commonly used to teach most subjects. *Practice and experience* are secondary. Test scores largely determine how much information a student can memorize and "play back."

If a student wants to perform in real-life situations, that will obviously require enough practice and experience to achieve what I call *Mastery*—being able to do something so well that you don't have to think about it. At that point a skill has become second nature. Ironically, that is the level of learning where many "learning-disabled" students excel when they really want to learn something and receive a form of instruction that works for them.

What Is Disability?

It is obvious that some students—about one in seven, as claimed by the U.S. Department of Education—have problems with assimilating information or acquiring skills in school. These students are usually labeled as "learning disabled." The word *disabled* means someone who is "physically or mentally incapacitated, or incapable of." If you add this definition to the one for learning, then we can say that *learning disability* means someone who is mentally or physically incapable of learning certain things.

Today, more than eighty different learning disabilities

have been defined and studied. The scientific and academic communities are busy publishing studies in journals that support various theories. When these make their way into the mainstream media, they are accepted by the public as "scientific truth." Yet there is such widespread disagreement that we are left to wonder: Which theory is true? What are we supposed to believe?

SCHOOLS OF THOUGHT

Currently, there are two basic theories about learning disabilities. In one camp are the geneticists who say it's all in the genes. In the other camp are theorists who study brain structure anomalies, which might be due to genetic mutations or birth defects. Both claim to have the answers.

Is It in the Genes?

Within the past ten years, four different studies were published by reputable researchers and universities that claimed to have identified the "dyslexia gene"—but each study claims it's caused by a different gene.

There is a growing body of scientific evidence that learning disabilities are inherited. I would say that is true of the *probability* of developing dyslexia or any of the other learning disabilities discussed in this book.

One convincing study of identical twins demonstrated that if one twin was dyslexic, the other was about twice as likely as normal to be dyslexic—but it wasn't inevitable. Identical twins are genetic clones, with *identical* gene structures. So this study would indicate that random developmental influences were about 50 percent responsible for the development of dyslexia during childhood—in other words, the cause of the dyslexia was about half hereditary and half developmental.

Is It in Brain Structure Anomalies?
Some theorists say the axons in the corpus callosum are too large; others say certain areas of the brain have too many axons or not enough; others say attention deficit disorder is caused by too few or too many receptors for certain neurotransmitters.

There have been studies comparing brain scans of dyslexics and non-dyslexics that suggest biological abnormalities, particularly in the left parietal lobe area. These scans have also shown underactivation in the posterior region of the brain, and overactivation in the anterior region when a dyslexic tries to read. But in my view, these studies don't address the effect disorientation can have on early childhood development, including the development of brain structure and function at an early age.

Over the past several years, researchers of child development have determined that our brains establish their basic programming before age three. Neural pathways that are stimulated develop; those that aren't used go dormant, and billions of unused brain cells simply atrophy through disuse.

Of course, we still wind up with a surplus of brain cells, and dormant neural pathways can be opened by stimulation throughout our lives. Otherwise, we couldn't continue to learn new things throughout later childhood, adolescence, and adulthood.

Who Is Right?

We are left with a dilemma: What *can* we believe? We have three choices. Either some theories are right and some are wrong, or all are wrong, or all are right. The "knee-jerk" reaction would be to say some are wrong and some are right. The cynical reaction would be to say they are all wrong. However, to say either of these would be a slur on the integrity of the scientific community, which I think is undeserved. The one thing we can say with certainty is the research is incomplete.

Let's assume all the scientific evidence is valid, if incomplete. In my view, both camps have largely ignored an important consideration—the developmental component. If we add it, we can see that these researchers have collected valid data, even if much of it, on the surface, appears to be contradictory.

If we consider that learning differences are usually accompanied by some special talents or special abilities, we have opened up the possibility that these students may also have a gift. They can do something that is considered "unusual" with their brains.

It doesn't make sense that a talent would be passed on by a single gene—that would probably require a "gene set." When learning differences are seen as latent talents that develop into multiple gifts, there would most probably be more than one gene involved.

As for structural anomalies, current studies from many different disciplines have found that the structure of the human brain is altered considerably through use during the first few years of life. Other studies show that the brain is far more adept at reprogramming itself throughout life than anyone suspected only a few years ago. So if we consider some of these brain anomalies as *effects* of how certain people use their brains rather than the cause, we can understand why these anomalies exist—in fact, they should be there.

Talents and gifts don't readily lend themselves to the scrutiny of the scientific method, so there may never be scientific proof of a "Gift of Dyslexia." Human diversity is unlikely to yield a one-size-fits-all DNA map of the dyslexic or ADD brain. However, there is empirical evidence that the learning and behavior problems associated with dyslexia and ADD can be corrected without physical or chemical intervention. It's relatively simple when we recognize and address a person's natural abilities and latent talents as avenues to overcome the difficulties that may accompany them.

A Broader Definition of "Dyslexia"

When we were developing strategies for working with the reading problems of dyslexia, we discovered two common threads that tied a broad range of learning disabilities together: *nonverbal thinking* and *disorientation.* Over the years, as we developed different strategies for correcting various learning disabilities, the theory underlying our work became known as the *Davis Theory.* Although we were addressing learning disabilities in general, we continued to use the word we had started with: "dyslexia." The problems of attention deficit disorder (ADD/ADHD), dyscalculia (math problems), and dysgraphia (handwriting problems) fall under the general heading of learning disabilities. On the surface these problems appear to be unrelated. However, twenty years of empirical evidence shows that not only are they related, they are actually different faces or facets of the same basic condition. For the most part they are simply different faces of dyslexia. It was this realization that allowed us to find the solutions contained in this book. Therefore, when you see the word *dyslexia* in the following text, its other faces of ADD, dyscalculia and dysgraphia are included in its meaning.

THE DAVIS THEORY

It is commonly accepted that human beings use two different types of conceptualization as part of our thought process—verbal and nonverbal. *Verbal conceptualization* means primarily thinking with the sounds of symbols and words; *nonverbal conceptualization* means primarily thinking with visual images.

Most adults use both types of thinking to some degree: They have learned to associate the sound of a word or its printed form with a mental image. But the verbal thinking method is a learned skill that cannot develop until the child has learned the language, and some children learn it later than others. Being born with the "Gift of Dyslexia" will usually delay the development of verbal conceptualization until at least age nine. So it's obvious that the nonverbal conceptualization thinking method, or "picture thinking," is more basic to human nature: All humans can do it from birth.

PICTURE THINKING

Since picture thinking is the type of thought addressed in the correction strategies laid out in this book, let's fully explore the process. We need to understand the anatomy of a mental image in order to understand exactly what is occurring.

If we consider that mental imagery is also called the imagination, and that there are no apparent limits to imagination, it might seem that mapping its anatomy would be impossible. In one respect, that is correct. With imagination, we could visualize a perfect world, or we could visualize the destruction of everything that exists. There is no limit to the significance of what we can imagine; it's boundless.

Limits of Picture Thinking

However, there are limits to the *mechanical* aspect of imagination. The limits of picture thinking aren't in the significance (meaning) of the images, but in their construction. A mental image can contain:

- a blank

- a color

- a variety of colors (even colors that do not exist in nature)

- a shape of any color

- a quantity of shapes of any color or many colors

- an odor or a variety of odors

- a taste or a variety of tastes

- a sensation or a variety of sensations (touch, balance, and motion)

- a sound or a piece of sound

- an emotion (feeling)

In essence, a mental image is much like a single frame of a holographic movie reel, except that it contains far more than just images and sounds. It also contains elements of the entire range of human perception. We call them mental "images" probably because the visual sense is the most profound, and we can recognize it as an image or picture. We're simply calling the whole package a mental "image" in order to give it a name.

There is another limitation that we must consider. Normally, nonverbal conceptualization is subliminal. It happens faster than we can be aware it is occurring. Using our imagination, we can slow the process down to see the images, or we may even be able to "freeze-frame" a single image. But at normal speed, we don't see anything. Conclusions and solutions seem to arrive intuitively.

It is very common for a person who primarily thinks in pictures to be unaware of what he or she is thinking about. It's common for a parent of a picture-thinking child to ask, "What are you thinking?" and get the answer "Nothing" or "I don't know." The "I don't know" answer is correct; they often don't have any idea.

Dyslexia and Picture Thinking

Dyslexics are primarily picture thinkers: They naturally think through mental or sensory imagery, rather than using words, sentences, or internal dialogue (self-talk) in their minds. Because this method of thinking is subliminal—faster than the person can be aware of— most dyslexics are not aware of what their minds are doing.

Picture thinkers tend to use global logic and reasoning, looking at the "big picture" when examining the world around them. They are usually very good at strategizing, creative endeavors, hands-on activities, and "seeing" solutions to real-world objective problems. But they don't do as well when they try to use word-based sequential, linear, step-by-step reasoning. When you look at a picture of a dog, you don't move your mind from tail to haunches to legs to shoulders to head to ears to nose in order to figure out you are looking at a dog. You see all parts at once and conclude "dog." If most or all of your thinking was done in pictures, you would become accustomed to figuring things out by looking at the whole object or situation at once, rather than analyzing, extrapolating, and then assimilating each piece of sensory data individually.

Picture thinkers also tend to develop very strong imaginations. They use a picture- or feeling-based reasoning process to solve problems rather than a verbal one. If they are confused (or intrigued), they will *disorient* in order to mentally turn an object around and look at it from different viewpoints or angles. By using this thought process, they develop many unique abilities and talents.

Picture Thinking and Disorientation

This ability can also be the foundation for a problem. When an individual becomes *disoriented,* his perception of the image or the reality at hand will become distorted. As we will discuss in the next chapter, anyone will experience a state of disorientation when looking at an optical illusion, or when exposed to misleading sensory stimuli. But many picture thinkers learn to use disorientation very early in life. It becomes their natural mental response to any confusing sensory information, as well as a method of creative problem solving. In the real world, it always seems to work.

But once a child starts school and tries to learn the symbols of language, disorientation becomes a hindrance. Because the child encounters so many sources of confusion in a single sentence, disorientations spontaneously occur, one after another. If the main problem is with reading, the child is labeled dyslexic. If the disorientation causes his sense of time to distort and his attention to jump around, he has ADD. If it affects math, he has dyscalculia. If it causes bad handwriting, he has dysgraphia.

When they try to interpret symbols that do not produce a mental image, dyslexics become confused and therefore disoriented. This leads to the familiar symptoms of substitutions, omissions, reversals, or transpositions in reading or writing letters, numbers, and words. It can also cause hyperactivity and difficulty paying attention. Following sequential instructions or performing sequenced mathematical operations may be impossible.

Disorientation is not limited to visual input; it can also cause a student to mishear or garble spoken words, or to alter the sequence of words in sentences. The disoriented person's sense of time can become inconsistent, and motor coordination may be delayed.

The repeated mistakes that result from misperceptions due to disorientation inevitably lead to emotional reactions, frustration, and loss of self-esteem. In an effort to solve this dilemma, each dyslexic will begin to develop a set of coping mechanisms and compulsive behaviors to get around these problems. We call these "old solutions." Some examples are rote memorization, the alphabet song, getting Mom to do the homework, acting out, illegible handwriting to cover up poor spelling, skillful deception, and avoidance of any task related to school or reading.

These can begin to develop as early as ages six or seven. By adulthood, a dyslexic may have a diverse, sophisticated repertoire of these behaviors. Now we can begin to see a full range of symptoms, characteristics, and behaviors commonly associated with dyslexia, ADD, and math and handwriting problems.

The most significant aspect of the Davis Theory in resolving dyslexia is the observation that when a symbol—a written word—lacks a mental picture and meaning for the dyslexic, disorientation and mistakes will result. When we show a dyslexic how to turn off the disorientations at the moment they occur, and then help find and master the symbolic information that triggered the disorientation, the reading, math, writing, and spelling problems start to disappear. So do the "old solutions," because they are no longer needed or useful.

CHAPTER 2

Orientation and Disorientation

The principle of orientation has to do primarily with perception. Our perceptions tell us where we are in our environment. A state of orientation exists when we are aware of our location and position. We achieve orientation by using all our senses of sight (visual), hearing (auditory), touch (tactile), smell (olfactory, including taste), balance and motion (kinesthetic), and time (temporal). Once we are aware of the location of things in the environment, based upon our perceptions, we can then place ourselves in the right relation to them. If you want to drive your car, you don't put yourself in the backseat. A state of orientation can exist only if and when the perceptions are accurate. Based on this principle, I would define *orientation* in this way:

n. 1. a state of existence where a person is accurately perceiving the environment. 2. an appropriate positioning of oneself within the environment. orient. 3. *(verb transitive).* an act of appropriately repositioning oneself within the environment. 4. an act of repositioning by oneself to achieve accurate perception.

The principle of disorientation is more complicated to pin down. It would be easy to simply say *disorientation* is the opposite of *orientation*. Based on the definition of orientation above, disorientation would be:

n. 1. a state of existence where a person is *not* accurately perceiving the environment. 2. an *in*appropriate positioning of oneself within the environment. disorient. 3. *(verb transitive)*. an act of *in*appropriately repositioning oneself within the environment. 4. an act of repositioning by oneself to achieve *in*accurate perception.

I don't want to make this sound more complicated than it already is, but I do want to make a distinction between simply being confused and actually experiencing distorted perceptions. For our purposes, we should narrow the scope of the term "disorientation" to include only instances where an individual's perceptions of the environment are inaccurate.

A Natural State of Disorientation

By defining orientation and disorientation we are implying that there is a natural state of orientation. This we have found to be true. However, it implies that everyone has a natural state of orientation wherein the perceptions are accurate. This, in fact, should not be assumed. Our research and experience has shown that natural orientation has two aspects: *consistency* of perception and *accuracy* of perception. A natural (or habitual) orientation does produce consistency of perception, but the perceptions may or may not be accurate. For most people consistent perception is reliably accurate enough to function—for them, their consistent perception seems accurate. For example, one person's perception of the color red may not be the same as another person's. In looking at the same red poppy, one person may see it as more orange and another as more purple.

EVERYONE DISORIENTS

Disorientation is not something only dyslexics experience. Most people have become disoriented from time to time.

For example, if you simply spin around fast several times and suddenly stop, you will be disoriented. Your vision will be impaired; the environment will still appear to be moving, and you will have difficulty walking correctly or standing upright, or "positioning yourself appropriately in the environment."

Another good example occurs when you are sitting in a stationary vehicle and something outside the vehicle moves, creating the false perception that you are moving. For instance, in a car wash, it's easy to get the sensation that we are moving as the jets of water cascade past the windows. The visual perception of motion causes a disorientation that in turn produces the false physical sensation of movement. The same thing can occur when stopped behind a car at a red light. You may feel that your car is moving forward when in fact, the other car in front is rolling *backward*. This false perception of motion is known as *Beta Apparent Phenomenon*.

We can also cause a state of disorientation with chemicals. Too much alcohol can cause the room to appear to be spinning, or distort our sense of time and speech. The alcohol causes disorientation, so the person no longer receives an accurate perception of the environment. This is why a drunken person staggers, or cannot balance on one foot, or possibly throws up.

Extreme emotions can also create a state of disorientation. Profound fear or extreme anxiety can disorient a person and cause a panic attack. Once the person is disoriented and his perceptions start distorting, he may actually see, as reality, things that aren't occurring. The sense of time will be distorted, as will many other perceptions such as motion and movement. Usually the person will experience a worst-case scenario of his fear.

We should also consider that there are degrees of disorientation. Spinning around doesn't always cause a person to fall down. Too much alcohol doesn't always cause a person to throw up. Fear doesn't always cause a full-blown panic attack. The disorientation that a dyslexic experiences can also vary to a similar degree.

THE DIZZINESS MACHINE EXPERIMENT
In 1982, I wanted to see whether the symptoms of disorientation would be any different in dyslexic and

Two hand-drawn spiral disks used
in the dizziness experiment.

non-dyslexic brains. I conducted a simple experiment whereby I mounted a spiral pattern on an old record player turntable, set it up on end, and then asked dyslexic and non-dyslexic people to stare into the spiral and see if they became disoriented. The symptoms were consistent. No one could tell how fast the disk was spinning. They all had trouble estimating the passage of time, repeating tongue twisters accurately, and maintaining balance. Many became nauseated.

My dyslexic students immediately recognized the distortions as similar if not identical to those they experienced when reading. One teenage boy became excited during the experiment and said, "That's it! That's my dyslexia! That's what it feels like when I have to read!" Later, after we had finished the experiment, he said, "I sure wish I could get my dad to come and sit in front of this thing. When he starts puking in that can, I could tell him he's just lazy!" Non-dyslexics, particularly parents, developed a profound appreciation for their children's problems from this experiment.

If you can relate to any of the above examples, then you can also appreciate what a dyslexic feels, sees, or hears during a state of disorientation.

Early in my research, it became obvious to me that all the symptoms of reading dyslexia were actually symptoms of disorientation. When a dyslexic individual is sufficiently confused, he will disorient spontaneously without noticing it.

But this is not the case with ADD and math and handwriting problems. For them, the effects of disorientation occur during early childhood development, long before a child is old enough to go to school. During childhood development, both the person's natural state of orientation and the mental function of disorientation, working together, distort some children's perception of their environment to the degree that they develop an alternate reality or concept of essential life lessons, such as *consequence*, *cause and effect*, *change*, and so on. The establishment of these alternate realities can lead to the development of ADD and, to some extent, problems with math and handwriting.

To have a solid foundation for this developmental theory, we need to explore further how disorientation can impact development.

Disorientation and Childhood Development

As we go through life, our experiences teach each of us the lessons necessary to continue living. As children, we learn the lessons necessary to live as adults. Because these lessons are experiential, the knowledge we gain becomes inherent within us. It becomes a part of who and what we are. It is the universal learning process.

It is through this learning process that we grow and mature. The principle is so natural that most people wouldn't even think to question it. But to understand certain learning disabilities, we must question its reliability. Several different factors can have an impact or influence this natural process in a negative manner to the point where it becomes a limiting factor.

THE IMPACT OF DISORIENTATION
ON A LIFE EXPERIENCE

If a group of people were to share the exact same life experience, each person would still learn a different lesson from it. The previous experiential knowledge of each individual has already formed a type of filtering system that interprets the significance of a current event. This in turn limits or influences our activity within a given environment.

For instance, when you were a child, maybe someone asked if you wanted to go for a ride on a roller coaster. You might have said yes or no. If you did take a ride, maybe you liked it, or maybe you didn't want to do it again. This series of responses resulted from the limiting factors of the filtering system that already existed within your mind. The experience, in turn, influenced your future behavior.

If we consider the impact of disorientation on a life experience, there is more happening than just a limitation from within the filtering system. There will also be an exception to the learning process itself, which in turn alters the filtering system.

We gain knowledge only from the life experiences that enter our awareness. We are aware of life experiences only because we perceive them—we see, feel, hear, taste, and smell them. If you slept through a mild earthquake, you wouldn't be aware that it had occurred. You wouldn't gain any knowledge from it, because you wouldn't have experienced it. But if the shaking woke you up, you would see, feel, and hear what happened. Not only would you be aware of it, but you would also gain some new knowledge from the experience.

So the reality of a life experience depends on it being perceived. The accuracy of the knowledge to be gained from a life experience depends on the accuracy of the perception.

Disorientation distorts perception. Distorted perception distorts our sense of reality. Therefore, disorientation produces a false, or alternate, reality of a life experience. A life lesson learned within an alternate reality is not going to be the same as one learned in an "oriented" state.

Short-Term Disorientation
We can easily see how this works when we look at the effects of disorientation on an individual with reading

dyslexia, because the mechanism is fairly simple. While reading, the person encounters words whose meanings cannot be pictured. These words produce blank pictures in the thinking process. The blank pictures contain a feeling of confusion. As the blank pictures accumulate, the feeling of confusion intensifies to the point where the person cannot tolerate any more confusion. At that point, a disorientation is stimulated, and the perception becomes distorted.

Then symptoms begin to appear—some letters may reverse, words may start moving, some words may disappear, or the letters and words may be reassembled into a different sequence. Actually, the only factor limiting these symptoms is the *imagination* of the disoriented individual. For a split second or a few seconds, the person experiences an alternate reality. The only possible lesson that could be learned from this experience is the product of the alternate reality induced by the symptoms. This is a negative effect of disorientation.

This type of disorientation also has positive effects. For example, disorientation can be useful for recognizing objects in the environment. The individual looks at something and fails to recognize what it is. This stimulates a momentary disorientation, and the person is able to see the object mentally from many different perspectives. It's a bit like rotating a 3-D model in a computer to look at its other sides. These different perspectives allow the object to be recognized, and then the disorientation terminates.

This type of disorientation is of very short duration.

It lasts only until the confusion is resolved, usually only a fraction of a second, although it may happen many, many times throughout the day. Even though the person experienced an alternate reality, the effect was positive because the object was immediately and accurately recognized. The life lesson learned from this experience is the ease of recognizing the object.

Now that we see how this works, we can ask, "How can disorientation create ADD and math and handwriting problems?" Just from these two examples, we can't formulate a complete answer yet. We will need to look deeper than the simplicity of the stimulus-response mechanisms that occur when recognizing objects and lead to the symptoms of reading dyslexia.

Long-Term Disorientation

Some disorientations don't switch on and off from moment to moment; they can continue for long periods of time. This type of disorientation can be measured in hours instead of fractions of seconds. During the disorientation the person is experiencing a long-term alternate reality. The person's alternate reality experiences have somehow excluded or missed important lessons that would prevent the unwanted behaviors of ADD, or concepts that would be needed to understand math. The most likely occurence would be that false or inaccurate concepts got installed into the person's filtering system.

Let's consider what it would take to prevent a child from learning just one of the basic lessons of life—*consequence,* meaning something that happens as a result of something else. If we consider that living involves experiencing a continuous series of consequences or results, how could someone not get it? It might seem that this basic lesson would be impossible to miss, unless the individual already has an alternate concept of consequence in place.

SELF-ENTERTAINMENT
Picture thinkers often indulge in long-term disorientation for the purpose of self-entertainment. Disorientation can throw the doors to inner fantasy wide open. A child may discover this capability while still an infant. With this discovery comes the alternate world of imagination and creativity, a world bounded only by the child's own intellect and limited only by his own creativity. To him, this is a world without bounds or limits—a world without consequences. The stream of consequences experienced by others in the real world is partly replaced by a continuous stream of creative imagination within the imaginary world, where he is the central figure.

Most everyone has experienced this sort of alternative reality during particularly vivid dreams. A picture thinker who uses imagination for entertainment has daydreams or "waking dreams" that are just as vivid. However they don't fit the model of an ordinary dream because the state of disorientation allows the dream to be experienced as reality. Disorientation also allows the person to interact with the alternate reality.

For a child who habitually spends much time in an imaginary world, nothing permanently exists. His friends and enemies exist only for him. The scenarios that are acted out are real only to him. To others, he is just playing by himself. To him it is his reality—his life. Even though he is just playing, the life lessons learned are incorporated into his filtering system. In his imaginary world consequence doesn't exist; things just happen—and almost anything can—at his whim and direction.

OTHER MISSING CONCEPTS
The concept of consequence isn't the only life lesson that can be replaced or altered by an alternate reality. Here is a list of some other missing concepts that are pertinent to learning problems:

Concept:	Real-life lesson:	Alternate-reality lesson:
change:	something becoming something else.	everything just is.
cause:	to make something happen.	everything just is.
effect:	something that is made to happen.	anything can happen.
before:	happening earlier.	only now exists.
after:	happening later.	only now exists.
time:	the measurement of change.	only now exists.

sequence:	the way things follow each other, one after another.	everything just is.
order:	things in their proper places, proper positions, and proper conditions.	things are where they are. things are how they are.
disorder:	things not in their proper places, or in their proper positions, or in their proper conditions.	things are where they are. things are how they are.

SELF-IMAGE

There is one more thing we need to consider. The child who has alternate perceptions of the concepts listed above may not have an accurate concept of *self*. He may not be able to perceive himself accurately in relation to others in his environment, like family members or acquaintances. He may not recognize that other people have feelings, needs, desires, or rights. These concepts simply may not exist for him.

At this point you should have a sufficient understanding of the concept of orientation and disorientation, and how these states can affect an individual's perception of his own environment. Using this model, we can see how the symptoms of various learning disabilities might develop. Let's apply this model to attention deficit disorder.

CHAPTER 3

Attention Deficit Disorder

Before we dive into the developmental aspect of attention deficit disorder, let me share with you a typical incident that illustrates the general lack of understanding about this condition. The two main characters in this scenario are a boy five or six years old who has ADD and his kindergarten teacher.

A Typical ADD Scenario

Our boy is a typical ADD child—intelligent, creative, imaginative, and hyperactive. He thinks primarily in pictures, and has already spent a lot of time using disorientation to entertain himself.

Our teacher chose her profession out of a profound love for children. But her crowded kindergarten class is quite a handful. Although she has tried hard not to make any judgments, she identified our boy as one of "those children" on the first day of school. He's a real live wire, and he doesn't listen to her. His behavior in the classroom makes an already difficult situation even worse.

The first few days of school are a difficult adjustment for all of the children, but most of them soon begin to settle down into the routine—except for that boy. If anything, his behavior is actually getting worse. He won't stay in his chair. He gets into everything.

The situation comes to a head during a morning recess. The teacher observes the boy push himself past six or seven other children waiting to climb the ladder of the slippery slide. He just bullies his way past the line of other waiting children, clambers his way to the top, and goes down in front of them. This shocks her. Not only is it rude, it's dangerous. She cannot allow this kind of behavior to continue.

The teacher grasps the boy by the shoulders as he heads back to the ladder to do it again. He tries to squirm loose, but she holds him firmly. She bends down, and in her sternest voice says, *"Look at me!"*

When he does, she says, *"What you did is wrong. You are supposed to wait in line until it's your turn! Do you understand me? You don't go down the slide until it's your turn!"*

The boy looks her straight in the face, nods his head, and says, "Yeah!"

The teacher lets go of the boy's shoulders and stands up. He immediately runs around to the ladder, pushes his way past several other children, climbs to the top, and goes down the slide.

This really upsets the teacher. Frustrated, she grasps

him again and marches him off the playground for a
"time-out" or whatever other form of discipline the
school is allowed to use.

The teacher is confused and not sure of what to do
next. The boy said he understood her and then did
exactly what she told him not to do. Without some form
of intervention, behavior modification, or perhaps a
medication like Ritalin, she cannot see any hope of
reaching this boy or imposing any control on him.

AN ANALYSIS

What just occurred confused the teacher. Her
conclusion seemed obvious to her based upon her
experiential knowledge and understanding of the
situation. True, based on her past experience or training,
behavior modification or Ritalin may be the only
solution she knows of for reaching this boy. But this is
not a real solution, because it does not address the real
problem. She doesn't comprehend that her own
misunderstanding of ADD might cause her to feel this
way. She feels the boy may have acted just to spite her.
Her conclusion seems logical, but it's incorrect.

In reality, based on the boy's tendency to think in
pictures, his experiential knowledge, and his limited
ability to understand what the teacher said to him, he
did exactly what she told him to do.

For our own understanding, let's consider that this
boy lacks accurate concepts of *self* and *change*. His
experiential knowledge of *consequence* is inaccurate,
and so are his concepts of *time, sequence,* and *order.*

He has either created inaccurate perceptions of, or

entirely missed, these concepts. In the alternate reality he creates by using disorientation, *change* occurs only at his whim, and there is no such thing as consequence. Simple ideas like "good" and "bad" are interpreted from this perspective. Good is what he likes; bad is what he doesn't like. Right is what he wants; wrong is what he doesn't want.

Without accurate concepts of *change* and *consequence*, nothing is permanent. Therefore, he has no concept of "before" and "after." His concept of time is elastic and unreliable in the outside world. Without the concepts of *change, consequence,* and *time*, the concept of *sequence* cannot exist. Nor can the concepts of *order* and *disorder*.

Word for Word

Let's consider what the teacher said to him, and interpret what his understanding of it might have been from a picture-thinking point of view.

She says, *"What you did is wrong!"*

He thinks:

- The word "What" has no mental image, so the word has no meaning for him.

- The word "you" means himself. His image for the meaning of this word is the same one he would get from looking in a mirror.

- He doesn't understand the word "did" for two reasons. First, it is the past tense of "do." He has no sense of "before" or "after," so past tenses don't register. Also, this is another word with no image, so it has no meaning to begin with. That word is just a blank spot in his mind, so he is left with only the mirror image of himself.

- The word "is" has no mental image of its own. Because it was preceded by the word "you," the mirror image of himself doesn't change.

- The word "wrong" has no meaning, except perhaps that the teacher doesn't like him. His mental image is now a picture of her holding him by the shoulders.

So the boy's understanding of this first sentence is a mental picture of the teacher holding him by the shoulders. His interpretation of the image would probably be, "she doesn't like me."

Then she says, *"You are supposed to wait in line until it's your turn!"*

He thinks:

- The word "you" brings another mental image of himself.

- The word "are" produces no image or meaning. The image of himself doesn't change.

- The word "supposed" produces no image, no meaning. No change in the image.

- The word "to" produces no image, no meaning. No change in the image.

- The word "wait" cannot be understood. Waiting is a function of time. The only concept of time he has is the present, so if he sees any image, it would be of the teacher holding him by the shoulders.

- The word "in" produces no image, no meaning. The image of the teacher holding him remains the same.

- The word "line" brings an image of a piece of paper with a line drawn on it. Now he sees an image of the teacher holding him, and a piece of paper with a line on it.

- The word "until" produces no image, no meaning. No change in the image.

- The word "it's" produces no image, no meaning. No change in the image.

- The word "your" produces another image of himself. No real change in the image.

- The word "turn," used as a noun, is a function of time, sequence, and order, none of which he is capable of comprehending. No image, no meaning. No change in the images of himself being held by the teacher and a piece of paper with a line on it.

At the end of this sentence, his mental images show the teacher holding him by the shoulders and a piece of paper with a line on it. His interpretation of the images would be that the teacher doesn't like him, or paper with a line on it.

She says, *"Do you understand me?"*

He thinks:

- The word "do" produces no image, no meaning.

- The word "you" again produces an image of himself.

- The word "understand" produces no image, no meaning.

- The word "me" produces an image of her holding him by the shoulders.

This sentence leaves him with only an image of her holding him by the shoulders. His only understanding is that she doesn't like him.

She says, *"You don't go down the slide until it's your turn!"*

- The word "you" brings an image of himself again.

- The word "don't" produces no meaning, no change in the image.

- The phrase "go down the slide" changes the image of himself to one of him going down the slide.

- The word "until" produces no meaning, no change in the image.

- The word "it's" produces no meaning, no change in the image.

- The word "your" simply reinforces the image of himself.

- The word "turn" produces no meaning, no change in the image.

The sentence leaves him with the image of himself going down the slide. His understanding is to go down the slide.

He says "Yeah!" in answer to this understanding, and promptly carries it out. Up the ladder he goes, pushing his way past the other kids as the teacher stares in disbelief.

A Two-Way Misunderstanding

What the teacher failed to realize was that the boy did exactly what he thought she told him to do, based upon his ability to understand what she said.

It's true that his behavior was rude and possibly dangerous. It should be effectively corrected. But neither a "time-out," detention, other forms of punishment, nor Ritalin will be capable of adding the understanding this boy needs in order to correct his behavior.

Understanding ADD

Before we consider how to correct attention deficit disorder, it would be helpful to learn what the medical establishment knows about it. *The Merck Manual* is a reference guide used in medical schools and by doctors. It lists and defines all known diseases, maladies, and conditions, and describes current diagnostic methods. The following excerpts have been taken from the fifteenth edition. I have included only those portions of the definition necessary to make our understanding as simple as possible, and have emphasized the parts pertinent to our discussion.

ATTENTION DEFICIT DISORDER (ADD)
(Hyperactivity; Hyperkinesis;
Minimal Brain Dysfunction)

Developmentally inappropriate inattention and impulsivity with and without hyperactivity. This definition conforms to the American Psychiatric Association's Diagnostic and Statistical Manual (DSM-III), shifting the focus of the disorder from excessive physical activity. Although the use of the term ADD (and others indicated in the synonyms above) as an independent diagnosis of a specific syndrome has been challenged, no study or critique has been able to discount the constellation of signs used to describe the disorder. ADD is implicated in learning disorders, and except for severe and profound mental retardation can influence the behavior of children at any cognitive level. ADD is estimated to affect 5 to 10% of school-aged children, precipitating half of the childhood referrals to diagnostic clinics. ADD is seen 10 times more frequently in boys than girls. *Etiology is* **unknown.** *Several theories advocating biochemical,* *sensory and motor, physiologic, and behavioral correlates and manifestations have been proposed.*

Symptoms and signs: The **primary signs** of ADD with or without hyperactivity are a child's display of inattention and impulsivity. ADD with hyperactivity is diagnosed when the signs of overactivity are obvious. Although children with ADD and without hyperactivity may not manifest high activity levels, most exhibit restlessness or jitteriness, short attention span, and poor impulse control. These are qualitatively different from those seen in conduct and anxiety disorders. **Inattention** is described *as a failure to finish tasks started, easy distractibility, seeming lack of attention, and difficulty concentrating on tasks requiring sustained attention.* **Impulsivity** is described *as acting before thinking, difficulty taking turns, problems organizing work, and constant shifting from one activity to another.* Impulsive responses are especially likely when involved with uncertainty and the need to attend carefully. **Hyperactivity** is featured *as difficulty staying seated and sitting still, and running or climbing on things excessively.* In general, children with hyperactivity are described as "always on the go."

. . . Diagnosis is often difficult. No particular organic signs of neurologic indicators are specific. Although organic factors may have a role in diagnosis, the primary signs are behavioral, varying with situation and time. Rating scales and checklists, the predominant mode of identification, often are unable to distinguish ADD from other behavioral disorders. Such data often are based on subjective observations made by untrained personnel.

As you can see, there is a lot of uncertainty surrounding both ADD and ADHD. It is difficult to diagnose; the cause (etiology) is unknown; and the people who provide the basic observations for a diagnosis are often untrained. While the medical profession can describe how a person with ADD behaves, they are still unsure as to what causes the condition and how to treat it without medication such as Ritalin. While Ritalin may alter the symptoms, it does not address the underlying nature of the problem.

ADD AND DISORIENTATION

The general definition of ADD is almost good enough: *developmentally inappropriate inattention and impulsivity with and without hyperactivity.* However, one component is missing: spontaneous disorientation. Disorientation is a major factor in the life of any person with ADD. It happens easily and often. It is usually driven by emotion. Boredom, curiosity, confusion, and fear are just a few of the emotions that can trigger an ADD disorientation.

In exploring spontaneous disorientation, I have found that these triggering emotions can be reduced to two types: avoidance and engagement.

In a boring situation, the person may disorient to avoid the boredom. This would be commonly recognized as daydreaming or simply as not paying attention. The student actually is paying attention, but has shifted it to an imaginary inner world that is more interesting.

On the other hand, we could have an instance where

something unexpected is introduced into the environment, like a motion outside the classroom window. Curiosity about such an event can stimulate a disorientation that will allow the person to explore the unknown event that triggered his curiosity. This is commonly recognized in school as inattention or distractibility. Again, there is no lack of attention; it is simply misplaced.

Disorientation caused by engagement can also create the opposite of inattention. The student may become so fixated on a given activity that he is oblivious to everything else in the environment. A person with ADD may disorient into a video game, TV program, or movie to the extent that the building could fall down around him and he wouldn't notice. Many parents of ADD children have told me that the teacher says their child can't sit still and pay attention for five minutes. Yet the parent cannot pry the child away from a video game for hours at a time.

To truly understand ADD, we must take into account the developmental track described in Chapter 2, which explains some typical behaviors like impulsivity, compulsivity, and disregard for the rights of others. We must also consider how in-the-moment, spontaneous disorientation can cause inattention, distractibility, and inappropriate responses to real-life situations.

EXAMINING ADD BEHAVIOR

Our understanding of the direct and indirect (developmental) effects of disorientation can explain all of the symptoms of ADD with or without hyperactivity.

From that understanding, we should be able to accurately define the condition as: *developmentally inappropriate inattention and impulsivity, with and without hyperactivity, accompanied by spontaneous disorientation.*

From this new understanding and definition, it is clear that this problem must be addressed from two fronts, because it was created by two contributing factors—the developmental component where alternate-reality life lessons are embedded into the filtering system, and recurrent episodes of spontaneous disorientation.

From an overview, correcting the problem means reducing or eliminating the undesirable behaviors by which it is recognized. These behaviors are:

- **hyperactivity:** *difficulty staying seated and sitting still, and running or climbing on things excessively.*

- **hypoactivity:** hypoactivity is not separately featured in *The Merck Manual,* but it can be interpreted as the aspect of ADD that occurs *without hyperactivity.* Kids with this type are often recognized as lethargic, daydreamers, lazy, or couch potatoes.

- **impulsivity:** *acting before thinking, difficulty taking turns, problems organizing work, and constant shifting from one activity to another.*

- **inattention:** *a failure to finish tasks started, easy distractibility, seeming lack of attention, and difficulty concentrating on tasks that require sustained attention.*

The Merck Manual gives us a description of what ADD is, but not an explanation of *why* or *how* it comes about. We can now explore that and determine whether these symptomatic behaviors result from the developmental aspect of the problem, the spontaneous disorientation aspect, or in some cases both. In doing so, we will explore the mechanics (how and why it happens) of ADD.

Hyperactivity and Hypoactivity

Both hyperactivity and hypoactivity are products of spontaneous disorientation, because every disorientation is accompanied by a shift in the perception of time. Biomechanically, our perception of time is a product of brain chemistry. There have been some studies that suggest that ADD children have elevated levels of dopamine. I believe this is a direct effect of disorientation.

The more dopamine around the synapses of the brain, the faster our "internal clock" will go. The opposite is also true: The less dopamine, the slower the internal clock will go. In cases where the dopamine production is chronically increased by disorientation, the individual will experience a faster internal clock speed, and vice versa.

Our perception of time passage is governed by the

*An hour of real time has passed. For the hypoactive
student on the left, it seems like only half an hour.
For the hyperactive student on the right, it seems
like two hours.*

speed of our internal clock. If the internal clock speeds
up, the clock on the wall will appear to slow down, and
vice versa. The faster we go inside, the slower the world
around us seems to go. In other words we have a
reversal of effect. Therefore, the hyperactive person
whose internal clock runs faster experiences *more* time
during an hour than the people around him. To the
hyperactive person, the world appears to be going too
slow. The reverse is also true: To the hypoactive
(lethargic) person, the world appears to be going too
fast.

The perception of having more time available than
other people does not in itself fully explain
hyperactivity. There is another piece to this puzzle:
Every disorientation also includes a reversal in the

senses of balance and movement. When disorientation occurs, we feel out of balance. If we are sitting still when it happens, we will feel as if we are moving, as explained in Chapter 2. On the other hand, if we are moving when the disorientation happens, we will feel as if we are sitting still, or moving slower or faster than we really are.

For many of us who experience this effect on a regular basis, we discover a simple remedy: By doing the opposite activity, we can reverse the effect. In other words, if we sense that we are moving when we aren't, we can create the sensation that we are sitting still by moving slightly.

When we do this, we are not consciously aware of the movement, and don't always need to show it. By fidgeting, bouncing a foot up and down, drumming hands, or another nervous activity, we can send a shock wave through our body that results in an overall sensation of sitting still. This remedy usually isn't discovered until a child is nine or ten years old. Before that, the false sensation of motion acts as a stimulus for body movement, which shows up as the "active" part of hyperactivity. When disoriented, the child is stimulated to be in a state of constant movement.

Many years ago, I had a student who was extremely hyperactive. His mother was at her wit's end with the boy, and I was attempting to explain how it happened. I had told her that her son could actually experience motion sickness if he were forced to be still when he was disoriented. She let me know that she found my explanation far-fetched. However, she agreed to let me perform an experiment on her son to demonstrate. I fashioned a "boat hat" from newspaper, but deliberately made it too small to fit well. In order to keep the hat on, he had to keep his head perfectly still. I taped a page of text on the wall at his eye level. His job was to keep the hat on while he stood there and read the text. The written text provided the disorientation. After several attempts with the hat falling off, he managed to get about halfway through the text before he vomited into a nearby wastebasket. His mother got the point.

The hyperactive component of ADD is clearly the product of two effects of disorientation: an increase in the speed of the internal clock and reversals in the senses of balance and motion. The hyperactive child has a lot of extra time, so he fills it up with extra activity. Hypoactivity is the opposite side of the same coin, where the reverse is true. The child has less time than other people, so he engages in less activity than the average person.

Impulsivity

For the most part, impulsivity stems from the developmental side of ADD, but not entirely. The component of *acting before thinking* is a manifestation of an alternate reality concept of *consequence. Difficulty taking turns* stems from a lack of the inherent concepts of *time, sequence*, and *order*. This has already been defined as developmental. *Problems organizing work* also stem from a lack of the inherent concepts of *sequence* and *order*.

Constant shifting from one activity to another is

more a manifestation of spontaneous disorientation. When a child has more time available than those around him he will easily become bored by the tempo of the environment. That, added to the stimulation for movement, produces what can appear to be a compulsive jumping from one activity to another. For the child, it feels normal.

Inattention

For the most part, inattention is a product of spontaneous disorientation, but not totally. The *failure to finish tasks started* is an interesting combination of causes and effects. Here, the effect of *impulsivity* or *shifting from one activity to another* shows up as the cause of failure to finish tasks. We consider this mostly a manifestation of spontaneous disorientation, but it is also caused by the developmental lack of the concepts of *consequence, time, sequence,* and *order.* The child may not be able to conceive of *finishing* anything because in his world that concept simply doesn't exist.

The *easy distractibility* component is, again, an interesting combination of factors. The child is more environmentally aware and more curious than other people. A child who is often bored may be easily distracted. But even when he isn't bored, something new entering the environment will immediately draw his attention. Even after the ADD is corrected, the person will still remain more aware and curious than others, so to a degree this behavior will continue. Once the child learns to multitask, he will be able to divide his attention between the two points of interest at the same time instead of shifting it back and forth from one to the other. This will relieve the teacher's burden somewhat, but the real solution would be to make what's happening in the classroom the most interesting thing in the environment for the student.

The wider view of distractibility is *difficulty concentrating on tasks requiring sustained attention.* Here *The Merck Manual* introduces new criteria— concentration and sustained attention. Concentration is performed by limiting awareness to one small area or endeavor. Sustained attention is simply the act of maintaining interest. As stated earlier, the ADD individual doesn't have difficulty "paying" attention as long as the task or activity is of interest to him. It's not his responsibility to make what the teacher is instructing interesting; that task belongs to the teacher. A widespread environmental awareness will naturally inhibit the ability to concentrate. Whether that is good or bad is a matter of opinion. Personally, I feel it's a great advantage.

Contrary to the myths promoted about ADD, the *seeming lack of attention* usually comes from the perspective of teachers and doctors who have mistaken the *shifting* of attention for *lack* of attention. If anything, the child already has more attention available than he needs. There is so much of it that he needs to spread it all over the environment.

In fact, there is so much available attention that nearly all ADD children will eventually learn to multitask. They do this by dividing their attention into two or more segments that appear to be simultaneously directed at different areas of interest. They will have to learn it on their own, because it's not a "subject" taught in school.

I think we could redefine "inattention." Instead of calling it *a failure to finish tasks started, easy distractibility, seeming lack of attention, and difficulty concentrating on tasks requiring sustained attention,* let's simply call it *difficulty staying on task.* It's a phrase familiar to teachers, and is something we can address.

We have just compared what *The Merck Manual* says about ADD with a new theory of why and how ADD symptoms come about. All the basic symptoms of ADD are addressed and explained by the new model. So it would make sense that correcting the condition should be possible.

Once you know the true nature of a problem, you can devise a strategy to address each of the individual components, one by one. Once you eliminate all the components, you have effectively eliminated the problem.

CHAPTER 4

Math Problems: Dyscalculia

The word *dyscalculia* means that a student has some difficulty in performing some aspects of arithmetic or mathematics. Another label, *acalculia,* means that a student cannot perform arithmetic at all.

As they are used by educators and educational psychologists, these terms describe problems in learning how to manipulate numbers in order to do addition, subtraction, multiplication, and division. Or they describe problems in studying or expressing the relationships between quantities and magnitudes, as represented by numbers and symbols.

A student with dyscalculia may make mistakes with simple problems and come up with answers like $2 \times 5 = 7$. Here the relationship to reading dyslexia is easy to see: Math symbols comprise a language of their own, so they can be misinterpreted or transposed just like alphabet letters. Another common symptom is reliance on finger counting or drawing hatch marks on paper instead of using numerals.

Often there are related problems in other areas. A

student who can't do math correctly may also have trouble with:

- right-left orientation
- following directions (such as maps or sequential instructions)
- learning how to tell time
- being on time
- musical notation
- physical coordination in sports or dance
- remembering events in the correct sequence

Math and Arithmetic

Before we begin to address these problems, we need to clearly define the terms *mathematics* and *arithmetic*. Contrary to common understanding, they are not the same thing. Mathematics is defined in *The New Lexicon Webster's Dictionary* as: n. *the science of expressing and studying the relationships between quantities and magnitudes as represented by numbers and symbols.* The same dictionary defines arithmetic as: n. *the manipulation of numbers by addition, subtraction, multiplication, division.*

This dictionary, which I consider one of the best, doesn't even make a connection between mathematics and arithmetic. It also says mathematics is a science when, in my opinion, it is only a tool used in science. The act of performing math, using arithmetic, is an art and not a science. Granted, the art form follows very strict guidelines, but it is an art nonetheless.

To help clarify the difference, consider that arithmetic principles are the tools used to *create* mathematics. Mathematics is the exploration of the unknown wilderness, and arithmetic is the tool kit you use to explore and map it. So, you actually perform mathematics by using the tools of arithmetic.

For a word-thinking adult these definitions are clear and concise. However, for a picture-thinking child, they can be like a solid brick wall, or a black hole in space. So I want to establish precise definitions for the two words that will be specific to our intention. For our purposes:

> **arithmetic:** *n.* a means of determining a quantity by counting or the manipulation of quantities, numbers, or numerals through addition, subtraction, multiplication, and/or division.

> **mathematics:** *n.* the art of determining quantities used in the science of studying and expressing relationships between quantities and magnitudes as represented by numbers, numerals, and symbols.

In these definitions, the purpose of both arithmetic and mathematics is the determination of a quantity. Here are specific definitions for some of the words within these definitions.

number: *n.* the amount present or considered.

numeral: *n.* a symbol representing a quantity.

quantity: *n.* actual amount, the number present or considered.

Numbers Versus Numerals

I have made slight changes from the common usage of these two words. Namely, I have made a clear distinction between a *number* and a *numeral*. In our society, they have become synonymous and are used interchangeably. But for the purposes of performing arithmetic and mathematics, we need this distinction. With this terminology, you wouldn't have a house number for an address; it would be a house *numeral*. The actual house number of a house with 231 painted above the door would only be the number *one*, because there is only a single house being identified with the numeral *231*. What is painted above the door isn't a number, it's a series of symbolic numerals.

DETERMINING QUANTITY
Another tricky part of this change has to do with the word *quantity*. A quantity can be realized simply by recognizing how many items are there, or it can be determined by *counting*. If two or three apples fall off a tree, most people will automatically know how many are on the ground. Once the number of apples on the

ground gets above an easily recognizable amount, things become more complicated. To determine the number, we would have to identify each one of the apples by using a numerical sequencing pattern.

Counting is the determination of a quantity through the use of a numerical sequence. This makes sense with real things and quantities, but if you start counting the houses on a given street until you get to a house with the numeral 231 painted on it, you will certainly come up with a different sequential number.

Picture Thinking and Math

A primary obstacle that prevents some students from learning math is the way the subject is taught. Typically, instruction is centered around language and verbal conceptualization. But arithmetic and mathematic principles and functions are not inherently linguistic; they are pictorial. They can be visualized very easily, even when the concepts are difficult to explain in words.

Although, as a child, I was labeled "retarded," I was able to produce the answers to complex trigonometry problems when I was around eight years old. At that time my mother was afraid I'd be labeled as an "idiot savant," so she insisted that I be removed from the classroom while the mechanics of arithmetic were being taught. This continued until ninth-grade algebra class, when I was allowed to attend a math class despite my mother's wishes. Although I was able to solve every algebraic equation, I still failed the class because I couldn't express how I got the answer. The teacher wanted me to do the arithmetic with a pencil using numerals, and I couldn't. It wasn't until I was fifteen years old, when a girlfriend taught me how to do arithmetic with a pencil, that I could show how to solve a problem on paper.

VERBAL AND NONVERBAL CONCEPTUALIZATION

Getting to the root of a math problem will require that we consider the variables that affect it. So let's briefly retrace some of the territory already covered. The main thing to consider is the two methods of thinking discussed in Chapter 1: *Verbal conceptualization* means primarily thinking with the sounds of symbols and words; *nonverbal conceptualization* means primarily thinking with visual images.

Reasoning Versus Seeing the Answer

Each of these two types of thinking can be used to perform the activities needed to determine a quantity. The verbal conceptualization mode of performing arithmetic uses *reasoning* to manipulate quantities through a series of remembered sequences. Essentially, the individual must mentally talk his way through a series of learned processes to determine an answer. As the arithmetic becomes more difficult, there will be more rules to remember and more steps to perform, with more different orders to establish and sequences to follow. By the time we get to three-place division, things become highly complicated.

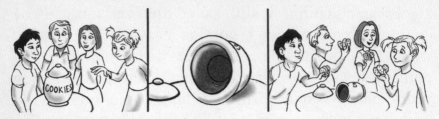

Math problems can be solved visually without going through the steps.

On the other hand, if the person is doing arithmetic pictorially, all that occurs is the manipulation of a series of mental images that result in the correct answer. Consider this simple problem: "If there are twelve cookies in a cookie jar and four friends are going to share them equally, how many cookies does each friend get?"

The word thinker might go through a process something like this:

1. twelve cookies

2. shared by four friends

3. each one gets the same amount

4. that means it's twelve cookies that are divided by the four friends

5. so, it would be twelve divided by four

6. so, twelve divided by four is three

7. so, each of the four friends gets three cookies each

8. so, the answer would be three

The picture thinker could experience a series of pictures that goes something like this:

1. a cookie jar with himself and three other children around it

2. then each child takes one cookie

3. then each child takes another cookie

4. then each child takes another cookie and the jar is empty

5. so he now has three cookies, and that's the answer

The word thinker is reasoning his way through the problem symbolically, while the picture thinker is subliminally recognizing a pattern of shapes and colors within mental images. In this example, the word thinker took eight steps and several seconds to arrive at an answer, while the picture thinker did it in only five steps and a fraction of a second.

From this example, the word thinker could explain and describe exactly how the answer was achieved. The picture thinker wouldn't even be aware of the images that were processed. It all happened so fast that he wouldn't be able to explain or describe any of it. If pushed for an explanation, probably the best he could come up with would be something like, "I only got three cookies." That isn't going to be an acceptable explanation to most teachers.

Both of these procedures are ways to solve a simple

problem, and both produced the correct answer. Picture-thinking students use a natural, visual-spatial method for performing arithmetic, but only the verbal thinking method will be acceptable in a classroom where math, engineering, science, accounting, or any subject involving arithmetic is taught.

Even so, the natural, visual method of doing arithmetic is the foundation upon which we must build. In using picture thinking, the person is thinking with the basic principles of arithmetic. The rules for doing arithmetic as it is taught in school are merely expressions of those principles reduced to language, so our final goal will be to help the student make this transition.

SYMBOL PROBLEMS

We must also keep in mind that some students aren't very good at thinking with the sounds of words, if they are capable of doing so at all. It is not natural for them to talk-think their way through any reasoning process.

It is just as difficult for them to visualize numerical manipulations, meaning to imagine doing the arithmetic by using numerals against a blank field, like a sheet of paper or a chalkboard. This may be difficult to understand if you are a word thinker, but the explanation is simple: To a word thinker, the words *number* and *numeral* mean the same thing. But to a picture thinker, a number is the quantity of actual objects. A numeral is only a symbol that appears on paper. It is easy to imagine an actual object because its significance is contained within it. This is not so with a symbol. The symbol has only an assigned significance that isn't inherent. The significance or meaning of the symbol must come from the person's memory.

Recognizing Quantities

To understand math, the visual aspect of the mental image is what we must explore. A mental image can contain a quantity of shapes. The shapes and colors of the shapes determine the identities of the elements. Suppose we look at a painting of a landscape containing trees, a lake, and a snowcapped mountain in the background. What distinguishes a tree from the lake and the mountain? It's the shape and the color that allows us to recognize that element of the picture as a tree.

How many trees are in the picture? That question really asks, how many elements in the picture do we recognize as being trees? Determining the quantity of individual elements is the essence of arithmetic. It is the basic principle from which all of the rules for performing arithmetic are derived. This is the beginning of truly understanding and doing math.

Effects of Disorientation

For someone who doesn't disorient, time passes by in a pretty uniform manner. Each second lasts as long as every other second. Minutes and hours also have uniform duration. Well before starting school, this person will develop an inherent sense of the passage of time.

Even though picture thinkers can think naturally with the principles of arithmetic, disorientation can still cause problems. Someone who disorients frequently can have difficulty with learning to do math in school because of the language and symbols that are used.

These problems can occur even if a child doesn't have long-term disorientations, or habitually daydream in an imaginary world. Even a few short-term disorientations per day may be enough to throw a student off, altering his experience of events that occur.

TIME VARIATION
Since disorientations cause a change in the perception of time, its passage doesn't seem uniform. This prevents the development of an inherent sense of time. Unless this area is addressed and corrected, many students will have difficulty with various aspects of time for their entire lives. The world around them seems to speed up and slow down in a way that is beyond their cognizance or control. This explains why students with math problems are also likely to have trouble with punctuality, following instructions, or any activity that involves following a sequence.

Inaccurate time perception will invariably cause problems with math, because a person without an inherent sense of *time* cannot develop an accurate concept of *sequence*. If the concepts of time and sequence are missing or inaccurate, the concepts of *order* and *consequence* will also be undeveloped.

Before, During, and After

The reason for this stems from the mechanics needed to perform arithmetic through logic and reasoning. All arithmetic and math problems ask students to determine the consequence of a specific action. Mechanically, all you ever do when solving a math problem is manipulate the concepts of time, sequence, and order to determine a result. For instance, if we start with six cookies and then add two more cookies, how many cookies do we have afterward? The consequence of two added to six is eight. What caused the number eight was the two extra cookies added to the original six.

Time as a Mathematical Concept

Consequence is actually determined through the concept of time—a change took place. For our purposes, time is simply defined as *the measurement of change according to a standard.* We don't really measure time itself with our watches and clocks; we measure change. The standards are based on the rotation of the earth and its orbit around the sun. All timepieces do is count in harmony with the standards.

So when two new cookies were put with six existing cookies, the measurement of the change is eight cookies existing together. Eight is the consequence of the change that took place. From this perspective, the answer to every math question is in the same form as time, because the answer is the measurement of the change.

Let's consider that same cookie example again and evaluate it in relation to the concepts of consequence, time, sequence, and order described in Chapter 2: "If we have six cookies and we add two more cookies, how many cookies do we have?"

Concepts

- consequence: *something that happens as a result of something else.*

- time: *the measurement of change.*

- sequence: *the way things follow each other one after another.*

- order: *things in their proper places, proper positions, and proper conditions.*

Evaluation

- Before: "If we have six cookies"—*order*—six cookies existing in the same place.

- During: "and we add two more cookies"—*sequence*—two cookies follow six cookies, and again, *order*—two additional cookies now also exist in that same place.

- After: "how many cookies"—*time*—measurement of change "do we have?"—*consequence*—two cookies added to six cookies causes us to have eight cookies.

The principle is the same whether we are calculating the orbit of an asteroid, the thrust of a rocket engine, or the quantity of cookies taken out of a cookie jar. At the level of mechanics, all these problems are solved using the same four basic concepts. Remove one or more of them, and you have removed the possibility of understanding how math works. Doing math will then be reduced to only the memorization of rote procedures, with no real understanding of its purpose.

Once your student is able to orient his perceptions at will, he will be able to master these basic concepts by creating them as scenarios with clay models. At that point, he will be ready to learn math principles visually, and finally make the transition to doing math by using numerals on paper. Then he should be able to perform normally in the classroom.

CHAPTER 5

Handwriting Problems: Dysgraphia

Until the typewriter was widely used, good handwriting was considered essential. Clerks and scribes wrote every legal and business document in impeccable script. People spent a lot of time and effort composing personal letters to friends and relatives. Now there is considerable debate as to whether or not good handwriting is relevant in today's world of computers, e-mail, and such. If a student can learn to use a keyboard and a spell checker, maybe that's enough to get by.

Handwriting is an art form that requires certain skills to accomplish. Some people may consider it dispensable in today's education process, but the education system still considers legible handwriting an essential element of the grade-school curriculum. A child with *dysgraphia* (difficulty writing) or *agraphia* (inability to write) is likely to be labeled "learning disabled" and sent to special education. I think most of us would agree that it is handy and valuable to be able to fill out paper forms, or to jot down a grocery list you

```
BJUYT KIOP M LKJHGFDSA:QWERTYUIOP;.-9BVBS4320W RT
                                            HA
                    HARTFORD, DEC. 9.
DEAR BROTHER:
I AM TRYING T TO GET THE HANG OF THIS NEW F
FANGLED WRITING MACHINE, BUT AM NOT MAKING
A SHINING SUCCESS OF IT. HOWEVER THIS IS THE
FIRST ATTEMPT I..EVER HAVE MADE, & YET I PER-
CEIVETHAT I SHALL SOON & EASILY ACQUIRE A FINE
FACILITY IN ITS USE. I SAW THE THING IN BOS-
TON THE OTHER DAY & WAS GREATLY TAKEN WI:TH
IT. SUSIE HAS STRUCK THE KEYS ONCE OR TWICE,
& NO DOUBT HAS PRINTED SOME LETTERS WHICH DO
NOT BELONG WHERE SHE PUT THEM.
THE HAVING BEEN A COMPOSITOR IS LIKELY TO BE
A GREAT HELP TO ME,SINCE O NE CHIEFLY NEEDS
SWIFTNESS IN BANGING THE KEYS.THE MACHINE COSTS
125 DOLLARS.THE MACHINE HAS SEVERAL VIRTUES
I BELIEVE IT WILL PRINT FASTER.THAN I CAN WRITE.
ONE MAY LEAN BACK IN HIS CHAIR & WORK IT. IT
PILES AN AWFUL STACK OF WORDS ON ONE PAGE.
IT DONT MUSS THINGS OR SCATTER INK BLOTS AROUND.
OF COURSE IT SAVES PAPER.
                         SUSIE IS GONE,
NOW, & I FANCY I SHALL MAKE BETTER PROGRESS.
WORKING THIS TYPE-WRITER REMINDS ME OF OLD
ROBERT BUCHANAN, WHO, YOU REMEMBER, USED TO
SET UP ARTICLES AT THE CASE WITHOUT PREVIOUS.
LY PUTTING THEM IN THE FORM OF MANUSCRIPT. I
WAS. LOST IN ADMIRATION OF SUOH MARVELOUS
INTELLECTUAL CAPACITY.
                          LOVE TO MOLLIE.
              YOUR-BROTHER,
                    SAM
```

In 1874, Mark Twain (Samuel Clemens) bought a typewriter for $125 and banged out an enthusiastic letter to his brother. Three months later, when the Remington makers wrote him for a recommendation, he replied that he had entirely stopped using it. He declared it was ruining his morals, because it made him "want to swear." Eventually, he traded it to a friend for a sidesaddle.

(From *Mark Twain: A Biography,* by Albert Bigelow Paine, Chelsea House Publishers, 1997) can read once you get to the store. An individual—child or adult—with dysgraphia or agraphia has a problem that is more than just an inconvenience. Even though some people may trivialize the problem, it can be a source of extreme embarrassment, and can contribute to lowered self-esteem.

Medical Definitions

For our purposes, we can simply define *dysgraphia* as *having some difficulty with penmanship*, and *agraphia*, the more severe form, as *the inability to write*. Here is a list of typical symptoms:

- Bad or illegible handwriting

- Awkward or cramped pencil grip

- Writing not going straight across the page even on lined paper

- Variations in the size of individual letters within a word

- Inconsistent in the way letters and words look (may print a certain letter different ways within the same document)

- Difficulty writing within the margins or line spacing and inconsistent spacing between words

In agraphia, the symptoms are the inability to hold and manipulate a writing instrument.

Now let's look at what medical science has to say about handwriting problems. My trusty *Merck Manual* mentions both *agraphia* and *dysgraphia,* but only within the description of *aphasia.* That condition is defined as: *A defect or loss of language function, in which the comprehension or expression of words (or nonverbal equivalents of words) is impaired as a result of injury to the language centers in the cerebral cortex.*

Injury to the inferior frontal gyrus just anterior to the facial and lingual areas of the motor cortex (Broca's area) produces an **expressive,** or **motor, aphasia** in which the patient's comprehension and ability to conceptualize are relatively preserved, but his ability to form language and express himself is impaired. Usually, the impairment affects both speech **(dysphasia)** and writing **(agraphia, dysgraphia).**

It is ironic that the medical profession, which is known for terrible handwriting, identifies brain damage as the cause of bad handwriting. Somehow it's difficult to believe that going through medical school could damage that many brains.

Even the National Center for Learning Disabilities defines dysgraphia as "a neurological disorder that involves writing."

We have discovered that handwriting problems are usually caused by several factors other than brain damage. By "brain damage," I mean any damage to the brain as the result of illness, trauma, or some genetic disorder.

Some aspects of this disability are easy to relate to reading dyslexia if you consider writing as the opposite of reading. When reading, the brain is seeing words on paper and converting them into concepts. When writing, the brain is taking concepts and converting them into words on paper.

In many cases, these problems clear up automatically as we solve reading difficulties, so it's very unlikely that brain damage was involved in the first place.

Also in many cases, even when there was existing pathology to prove brain damage, we have had success addressing handwriting problems. We produced improvements in handwriting that were undeniable and permanent. We obviously could not have repaired the actual brain damage, so my best guess is that new neural pathways were opened to skirt around the area of damage. This would be similar to what happens when occupational therapists help people regain motor skills after strokes or accidents.

Seven Causes of Handwriting Problems

Every handwriting problem has two elements: specific skills that are missing, and the reason those skills haven't yet been developed. When we observe someone's problem, all we're looking at is the absence of skills. We must look at the person—the individual himself—to find why they didn't develop. In working with students over the years, I have distinguished seven possible reasons why a person might have a handwriting problem:

- brain damage
- physical illness and deformity
- intentionally poor penmanship
- no or inadequate instruction
- disorientation
- multiple mental images
- an inadequate natural orientation

Not all of these are related to dyslexia, so we won't be able to directly address every one of them—only the last four in this list. Dealing with the first three causes is beyond the scope of this book, so I'll only provide a brief overview.

BRAIN DAMAGE

Brain damage might be the result of a birth defect, an illness, or an accidental injury. If there is actual brain damage, there will be pathology to support its existence. I don't mean a suspicion that a child *might* have fallen off the swing set. I mean documented complications at the time of birth, or of a high sustained fever, an accident that resulted in head injury, or a near drowning.

We don't have a uniformly effective strategy, but we have achieved limited success by addressing the problem in the same way we do for *dyspraxia* (the clumsy form of dyslexia, or inadequate natural orientation). Follow the strategy and instructions laid out in Chapter 24 and see what happens.

PHYSICAL ILLNESS AND DEFORMITY

Physical deformity could also be the result of a birth defect, an illness, or an accidental injury. The deformity will usually be obvious. However, this category also includes medical conditions such as cerebral palsy, muscular dystrophy, multiple sclerosis, and infantile paralysis. For these, there should be a medical history to document the condition. Handwriting problems that accompany physical illness and deformity are outside the scope of our strategies.

INTENTIONALLY POOR PENMANSHIP

Intentionally poor penmanship is a common reason for poor handwriting. There is no direct link to dyslexia. Anyone can acquire this habit, most likely to hide some other deficit. Often, the person tries to hide poor spelling behind poor handwriting. Poor handwriting could also be used to conceal uncertainty on punctuation, grammar, or sentence structure. If the reader is struggling to decipher the scribble, maybe they'll overlook a misspelled word or two, or won't notice the lack of commas and periods, or that no words are capitalized. After awhile, the habit becomes ingrained, and the person may not even be aware that this is what they are doing.

In general, intentionally poor handwriting doesn't have any specific symptoms, so identifying it can be tricky. You could look for an underlying problem that is being hidden by checking the spelling, punctuation, and grammar skills, but even then you might have a hard time. Probably the best way to identify it is through the process of elimination. If the problem doesn't fit into any of the other categories, then you can conclude that this is the problem.

Intentionally bad handwriting doesn't have a direct link to picture thinking or disorientation, so we won't pursue it any further or propose any direct solutions.

However, if you are dealing with a child who has been diagnosed with ADD, you might see a handwriting problem that *looks* intentional, but isn't. In this case, the child's writing is normally indecipherable, but if pressed, he can write quite legibly. This can be frustrating to a parent who knows the child can do better, but won't. It almost seems as if the child is lazy, doesn't care, or is just being insolent. For the most part, this problem is related to the speed of the internal clock. It seems almost miraculous, but with the simple tools of Orientation (Chapter 9) and the installation of an Energy Dial (Chapter 13), the problem should disappear on its own.

NO OR INADEQUATE INSTRUCTION
This one is so obvious that it's easy to overlook. A student may have a handwriting problem simply because he was never given proper instructions in penmanship, or the instructions weren't sufficient to build the necessary skills. Not everyone in the world gets to go to school. Sometimes severe childhood

illnesses interfere with school attendance, so important classes are missed and never adequately remediated.

These deficiencies are not directly related to picture thinking or disorientation, but disorientation can indirectly contribute to the problem. The ability to disorient allows the student to be physically present in a classroom without being there mentally. An alternate reality or daydream produced by a disoriented state will undermine even the best instruction. And there may be another link.

Over the years, I have worked with a number of older students who were identified as being dyslexic in kindergarten or first grade. As part of the school's attempt to provide an adequate education as required by law, concessions were made. These often included one-on-one or small group instructions for reading. These special instructions weren't given in addition to regular classroom activities, but *in place of* them. By third grade, these students were put into a special education program that consisted mainly of phonics-based reading instruction. A number of them told me that they cannot remember ever having been given any instruction in penmanship.

To determine whether your student's problem fits into this category, start with an interview: Ask the student if he was given adequate instructions. If not, the solution is simple and straightforward—provide them. However, if the student wasn't given adequate instructions because of "special education," there will probably be other learning problems that need to be resolved first.

DISORIENTATION

This category follows the same stimulus-response model as reading dyslexia. The individual, in an oriented state, encounters a stimulus and becomes disoriented, usually for only a split second. During the disorientation, the handwriting goes askew. We have found this particular problem to be rare in children, and then almost always accompanied by reading dyslexia.

Over the years, we have found that the handwriting disorientation triggers fall into two basic categories: *line and shape triggers* and *motion triggers.* Neither lines, shapes, nor motions by themselves can cause disorientation, so there must be something in between the trigger and the disorientation. It is emotion. For reading dyslexia, the triggering emotion is the feeling of confusion. For the handwriting problem, it could be confusion or something else.

So, we have the anatomy of a trigger—line, shape, or motion—which produces an emotion, which in turn causes disorientation. Emotions actually come from the individual's life experiences. Somewhere in the person's past is a real-life experience that contained that emotion. Somehow, a line in a particular direction, or a certain shape, or a particular motion reminds the individual of that experience. Subconsciously linking the line, shape, or motion to the past experience brings the emotion forward in time. The individual begins to unconsciously experience the past emotion in the present, and the result is a disorientation.

To recognize this type of problem, watch the person write. You will see disorientation symptoms that usually last for only a fraction of a second. The disorientation will cause a consistent anomaly or "glitch" in the handwriting caused by a tic or twitch in the muscles. Every time the student must draw a line in a particular direction, there is a disorientation and the anomaly occurs. Or every time the student must draw a particular shape, or move the hand or pencil in a particular motion, there it is. It will happen in the exact same place and in the same configuration every time it occurs.

The glitch will appear in the formation of the line or shape the student is trying to draw. For example, the circular shape of the letter O may not be round; it may look like a D or have wavy vertical lines.

A student in this category will often develop micro-writing, where the writing is tiny. He will find it difficult to make the letters larger.

Another possibility is a student with reading dyslexia who experiences an overall confusion with words. In this situation, the mere act of writing words becomes the trigger for disorientation. Here are two common characteristics that identify this problem:

- On unlined paper, the writing doesn't go straight across the page. Sometimes even on lined paper it may not be straight.

- Usually the size of the letters isn't consistent, especially in block printing. There may be an inappropriate mixture of upper- and lowercase letters. With older students, the writing may be limited to block printing in uppercase.

If this is the case, correct the reading dyslexia before you address the handwriting problem. In the process, the handwriting problem may disappear without further instruction. If it doesn't, there are specific exercises in Chapter 22 to identify and desensitize the triggering emotions.

MULTIPLE MENTAL IMAGES

Disorientation isn't a direct factor here, but simply being a picture thinker can make a person vulnerable to the problem. It is created when a penmanship teacher doesn't understand what can happen when visual models are given to a picture thinker. In the process of giving the student instructions, the teacher inadvertently gives the student multiple models of what writing should look like. For instance, a kindergarten student named John is learning to write his name in the school's approved writing format. He draws:

The student didn't quite get it on the first try, so as a model, the teacher draws the word correctly to the left of the one the student has drawn.

The student tries again.

It's still off a bit, so next to that the teacher draws another example.

What the teacher is doing seems reasonable. The student is given models to follow and duplicate. The problem is the two models the teacher provided are not identical.

This wouldn't be a problem for most students, but for a picture thinker it can create *agraphia*, the most severe of all writing problems.

The picture-thinking student made an exact mental

copy of the teacher's model. When the second model was given, the student made an exact mental copy of that one as well. The next time he tried to draw the word, he mentally looked at both of these mental pictures, but not side by side. The pictures were superimposed on top of one another. The models weren't identical, so the mixture of the shapes of the lines formed a snarl of multiple lines. The mental picture the student tried to follow was impossible to draw.

In a situation like this, every time the teacher provides another model, even with very slight variations, the new model adds more difficulty as it is superimposed on the others. Literally, the more instruction the student receives, the worse the problem becomes. The more models he is shown, the more difficult it becomes for him to even attempt to write. He ends up with a mental picture that looks like this:

As a natural reaction, the student will begin to grip the pencil tighter and tighter until his fingers are fatigued. He will press harder and harder with the pencil until the lead breaks or the paper tears. With each attempt he makes simply to write his name, his entire body will become more tense. Eventually, he will get to the point where he can't even hold and manipulate a writing instrument. The mere thought of attempting to write could cause extreme anxiety. It's quite common for children with agraphia to be taking prescription medications for the symptoms of hypertension, depression, or ADD.

These signs indicate that multiple mental images need to be addressed.

INADEQUATE NATURAL ORIENTATION *(DYSPRAXIA)*

Finally, we have the handwriting problem that accompanies the condition known as *dyspraxia.* Dyspraxia is most commonly associated with an "auditory deficit disorder," but we also see it as "clumsy child syndrome." It affects between 2 to 4 percent of the population, and is generally considered a neurological deficit that delays or prevents the development of motor skills and coordination. Poor handwriting is only one of many possible symptoms:

- Overall poor coordination. The person is clumsy, and may have a hard time walking evenly, tying shoes, or performing any task that requires fine motor skills.

- Lack of lateralization (right-left sense). The person has difficulty distinguishing right from left and with crossing the midline of the body with either hand or foot.

- Perceptual and speech difficulties. The person may have problems understanding what was said, or may have a speech impairment.

Researchers have noted that this condition is often *accompanied* by dyslexia, ADD, dysgraphia, or math problems. We simply call it "the clumsy form of dyslexia."

We have found that dyspraxia occurs when a person's natural orientation is in a very unfavorable place. Their habitual orientation is somewhere in front of the body and below the line of sight. This orientation will produce the classic symptoms of mixed hemispheric dominance of the brain, such as right-left confusion. It can also create the effect of a midline barrier, where the individual cannot move a hand or foot across the midline of his body.

The midline barrier also prevents the eyes from scanning across the midline, so it can be a barrier to perception. For such a person, half of the world is cut off. For them, the half of the world on the other side of the midline barrier simply does not exist. This anomaly doesn't affect only visual perception; it also severely distorts auditory perception so that the person may hear sounds as garbled, too loud or soft, or coming from the wrong place. This explains why the problem is often seen as an auditory deficit.

In students who have reached the age where motor skills would normally be developed, the symptoms of the midline barrier are easy to see. When they talk to you, they usually don't look directly at you. If they do, one eye will often close or veer off in a different direction. They are almost always heavy on their feet and extremely clumsy. When they read, they hold the book off to one side, sometimes at a ninety-degree angle. When they try to write, the paper is also placed off to one side. Often they angle the paper so their writing is vertical instead of going from left to right.

The handwriting problem that accompanies the midline barrier occurs primarily when the student must draw a letter that would cross the midline, but the problem goes way beyond that. When we look straight at a block-print capital letter A, we see the symmetry of the letter. The diagonal lines are straight and meet in the center at the top. The horizontal line is straight, and links the two diagonal lines at their centers. A person with a midline barrier can't look straight at the letter; he would only be able to see half of it. To see the entire character, he needs to shift the point of focus so the entire letter is on one side of the midline. In doing this, he loses the symmetry of the letter. The diagonal lines appear to be curved, and don't appear to meet at the center of the character. The handwriting problem is caused by the perception problem. When attempting to draw the letters, the very best that can be done is to duplicate the perceptual distortions.

Taking an overview of this situation, we can conclude that the brain of this individual has never seen straight vertical or diagonal lines. The inability to look straight at them has caused a perceptual distortion. If the brain has never seen them, it cannot instruct the hand to draw them.

Even with years of practice, someone with dyspraxia won't be able to draw a straight vertical or diagonal line until they learn orientation. Turning the paper ninety degrees to write up and down helps a little, but still doesn't eliminate the need to the draw vertical and diagonal lines.

A dyspraxic child who is being taught penmanship has a handicap that the teacher doesn't see or understand. Because the child cannot see the symmetry of any of the letters, no amount of traditional instruction in writing will ever make a difference. It doesn't matter how many models of what the writing *should* look like are shown to the student. His brain cannot accurately perceive the model images, so he will never get it right.

This writing problem is not limited to the inability to draw straight vertical or diagonal lines. Intersecting lines present an even bigger problem. The child will have extreme difficulty with letters that contain intersecting diagonal lines, like the letters A, M, V, and W, because the lack of symmetry distorts the perception of the intersecting points. The A and V are difficult enough with only one intersection. The M and W, having three, are unbelievably difficult.

Identifying this category of problem is easy, because you will see many of the obvious characteristics described above. To narrow it down further, you could simply ask the student to draw the block-print uppercase letters A and W, following a model. Better yet, to avoid confusion with the multiple mental image category, ask the student to fashion the letters A and W using clay "ropes" by copying a model you make on the table. If the problem is dyspraxia, there won't be any symmetry in the letters. The lines will not be straight, and the intersecting points will be incorrect. It might look something like this:

That pretty well covers all the possibilities. If your student has a handwriting problem, the probable cause should be one of the categories described above. Over the years, we have developed corrective strategies for the last four, all of which relate directly or indirectly to disorientation and picture thinking. The strategies in Chapters 20–24 are our time-tested techniques for eliminating them.

SECTION TWO

The
Basic
Tools

CHAPTER 6

Introduction to the Basic Tools Package

The basic Orientation Counseling and Symbol Mastery procedures used in this book are the same as those published in our first book, *The Gift of Dyslexia*. This book includes three additional procedures pertinent to working with the other facets of dyslexia that were not previously published. All of these comprise a "basic tools package" that is used in addition to the specific exercises for correcting ADD and math and handwriting problems. The introduction to each section on these specific learning problems will tell you which of the basic tools exercises to perform, and in what order. Here is a brief overview of the basic tools that follow:

Chapter 7: Motivation and Responsibility

The first step in correcting any learning disability is the desire for a change. This chapter gives you guidelines and pointers to assist your student in finding and developing the motivation necessary to address a learning problem.

Chapter 8: Perceptual Ability Assessment

There are two procedures that can be used for bringing about an orientated state—Orientation Counseling and Alignment. This brief evaluation will tell you which of the two is most appropriate for your student's preferred thinking style. If your student can easily perform the steps of the assessment you'll use Orientation Counseling; if not, you'll use Alignment.

Chapter 9: Orientation Counseling

The original Orientation procedure establishes an orientation "point" that enables a student to perceive the physical environment without perceptual distortions. This procedure is most appropriate for individuals who are primarily visual learners.

Chapter 10: Release and Review for Orientation Counseling

Release is a relaxation exercise that enables a student to prevent or eliminate stress and tension. Review is a simple method of checking the position of the orientation point for the first few days after the initial Orientation session.

Chapter 11: Fine-Tuning for Orientation Counseling

Here, you will help the student find the optimum orientation point, and learn to periodically readjust it.

Chapter 12: Alignment Procedure

Alignment is an orientation technique for individuals who are primarily kinesthetic or tactile learners, or are below the age of seven (see Chapter 12 for more detail). If your student can't easily perform the Perceptual Ability Assessment exercise, this is the form of orientation to use.

Chapter 13: Energy Dial Setting

This is a mental process that enables a student to control his internal time clock and adjust his energy level to a "setting" that is appropriate for a given activity. This procedure was developed to help students control the "hyper" aspect of ADD, but we have found it beneficial for all students, with or without learning problems.

Chapter 14: Coordination Therapy

If your student has any symptoms of clumsiness, poor coordination, or delayed development of motor skills, use this simple exercise periodically after Fine-Tuning.

Chapter 15: Symbol Mastery and Concept Mastery

In Symbol Mastery, the student models the meaning and configuration of the symbols of language from clay. The symbols are basic alphabet, punctuation or numeric symbols, or words. This is a way to connect symbols with their meanings, or significance. If your student has symptoms of reading dyslexia, you will probably want to go through the complete correction program laid out in *The Gift of Dyslexia*. Here, we have provided a general description of the Symbol Mastery steps for the alphabet, punctuation marks, and words.

In Concept Mastery, the student creates a scenario from clay that demonstrates a basic concept or principle needed as a foundation for learning. The creation will include the concept of "self." This is done so the student can examine how the principle or concept relates to him, and how he interacts with his environment and other people.

Chapter 16: Establishing Order

Children (and many adults) with ADD are notoriously disorganized and disorderly. The same is generally true of people with math problems. Disorderliness relates to many aspects of the condition, including poor time sense and a lack of understand of basic concepts such as consequence and sequence. Once you have dealt with these concepts, it may be time for some practical exercise in the basic principles of establishing and maintaining order. These exercises are also designed to foster personal responsibility. You can use them with anyone who needs to gain the ability to establish and maintain order.

Which Orientation Method to Use

The first step in doing the basic procedures is deciding which orientation method to use. Here are some guidelines:

- If you're working with a child under the age of seven, use the Alignment procedure. It has been proven effective with children as young as five.

- If you're working with a child seven or older, do the Perceptual Ability Assessment. If the person can easily visualize a piece of cake in his hand, and view it from different perspectives, use Orientation Counseling.

• If the person can't easily do what is requested in the Perceptual Ability Assessment, you are most likely dealing with a tactile or kinesthetic learner, so use the Alignment procedure.

Orientation Counseling is the best procedure for someone whose learning style is primarily visual. However, some dyslexics are primarily tactile learners, and a few may even be primarily auditory learners. For them the Orientation procedure may be difficult or impossible to do. That doesn't mean they cannot experience an oriented state, or learn to control disorientation; it only means they need a different way to get there.

At face value, one orientation procedure isn't superior to another, because the end result for each is a person who can produce an oriented state at will. The difference is ease of application. The easier it is for someone to use a tool, the more effective the tool will be for that person. That's why there are two to choose from.

Studies of the Davis Learning Strategies Program, a classroom adaptation of the Davis Methods, have shown that all younger students benefit from having an orientation tool, whether they have learning problems or not. The K–3 students in the study were given a procedure called *Focusing*, a variation of the Alignment procedure that is led by the teacher as a group activity.

USE ONLY ONE PROCEDURE
It might seem logical just to give the student both procedures and let him determine which is best, but

there is a flaw in that simple logic. It would be like giving an aspiring lumberjack an ax in one hand and a chain saw in the other, and asking him to fell a tree. He could probably do it with either tool, but not if he tried to use both tools at the same time. He would wind up hitting the chain saw with the ax or hitting the ax with the chain saw. Neither tool would be effective, and either one could be damaged. Of course, the ax and the chain saw are physical tools. You can keep them in a toolbox and only take one of them out at a time. The orientation procedures are mental processes that cannot be easily separated.

Experience has taught us that when an attempt is made to use both tools at the same time, the student may experience unpredictable perceptual distortions. If this happens, it can be difficult to undo, and the student may be left with an aversion to using either tool.

THE MIND'S EYE

Whether you use Orientation or Alignment, you will be asking the student to mentally perceive the world from a particular point in space and establish a "point" or optimum location. This concept isn't always easy to grasp for people who aren't dyslexic, because they already habitually perceive the world from a fixed point of orientation. It may not be entirely accurate, but it's stable. A dyslexic who has learned to use disorientation early in life tends to shift his orientation around in order to perceive the world in different ways.

Most people seem to have the sense of perceiving the environment from somewhere behind their eyes. For verbal thinkers, the location they are looking out from is often a stable point somewhere inside the back of their head.

Wherever it is, this location is what I originally termed "the epicenter of perception" or, for short, the mind's eye. It is the imaginary place in space from which a person receives most perceptual stimuli— including sound, balance and motion, and retrieved mental images.

For dyslexics, who spontaneously form a 3-D mental model of the world around them, the mind's eye relocates in order to capture different perspectives. When a dyslexic mistakes the letter *b* for a *d,* it's likely that the letter is being viewed from behind—the mind's eye jumped to the other side of the paper. This comes in handy when dealing with 3-D objects, but in order to see two-dimensional symbols accurately, the mind's eye needs to be stabilized in a place where the perceptions are consistent and accurate. That is all orientation does. We establish a mental viewpoint in space where perception is optimum. This point is typically six to twelve inches above and behind the head. It is always on the midline of the body.

From reading the descriptions of the two procedures, you can see that both are designed to achieve the same result. The subsequent fine-tuning exercises simply help the person find the precise location where all the perceptions are "tuned in" for maximum accuracy.

Once you have completed all the steps of the appropriate orientation procedure, you can zero in on the area of learning that presents the biggest obstacle for your student. Hopefully, you have gained a good understanding of what to work on by reading the previous chapters. So once you have the student's agreement, simply follow the instructions like a recipe. If you're on the right track, you should see positive results from the start.

A Mom's Advice

(This letter was originally posted on the Davis Dyslexia Association discussion board at www.Dyslexiatalk.com)

I went through the orientation counseling with my daughter. She was almost thirteen at the time and we were both amazed! I didn't understand it, but she did! If you yourself are not dyslexic, it will probably be impossible to fathom that it will work.

The book's outline worked perfectly for us. Just follow, step-by-step, don't leave anything out—and it will work for the student. Be very confident.

I was floored! My daughter was able to visualize everything just as the book was showing, and I (with disbelief sometimes) just kept going till we were all done.

Find a quiet place where there are no distractions, no phone calls or doorbells, no dogs barking. Allow two hours to get through the Assessment and Orientation. This will give you time to take breaks and to practice Release, too, if necessary.

When we were all done, my daughter was practically bouncing off the walls, she thought it was 'so cool!' I wish I could know what she felt. Guess I don't have that exceptional, imaginative, three-dimensional mind that she does.

This is a good example of 'do first, ask questions later.' Good luck to anyone who uses this—don't be afraid, just do it!

—Connie Kronberg-Talbert

CHAPTER 7

Motivation and Responsibility

These are the two key factors you will need to address before you take on the job of correcting any learning disability. There is a simple truth that can't be overlooked: The only person with the potential for correcting a learning problem is the person who has it. Your role as a helper or mentor is only to facilitate the other person's efforts to make the necessary changes. You cannot do it for him, nor can you do it to him.

The tools in this book will work only if you have the willing cooperation of your student. If he doesn't have a sincere desire for change, your chances of success in facilitating the correction of the problem are very slim. If he isn't motivated, you will only waste your time by trying to make him change. So the step of motivating the student is the most important of the entire process.

The success of a correction process is keyed to the placement of responsibility. By this I don't mean "burden" or "liability" or "obligation." The essence of responsibility is *the ability and willingness to control something*. A state of responsibility can exist only when a person is able *and* willing to cause a desired change or to prevent an undesired change. If someone is able but not willing, he cannot be responsible. Likewise, if he is willing but not able, he cannot be responsible. Whenever we seriously violate this simple concept, we can expect emotional and psychological trauma. If you want to experience what it feels like to be insane, try to be responsible for something you aren't able to change. The feelings of frustration and guilt are products of violated responsibility.

The proper perspective, then, is to assume that the person you are working with must be given, and must accept, responsibility for correcting his own learning problems. At the start, your student will lack the knowledge and skill to do so. So your first job is to help your student become willing to assume responsibility for correcting the problem. Then you can help him gain the knowledge and skill that is needed to do so.

This book will provide the particulars on what to do. As you help the student put the information into practice, it will become his knowledge. With a little practice using the new knowledge, his skills will develop naturally. Your job is to assist the person by giving him the instruction and tools that will enable him to gain the knowledge and skills he needs.

Your Own Responsibility

Your job as helper has its own responsibilities. You must be able to read and follow the instructions. You must be willing and able to assist the student with instructions on what to do. You must also be able to give those instructions without infringing on the other person's responsibility.

Most important, your job is to make sure the student is motivated to eliminate the problem. If the student isn't properly motivated or willing to be responsible, you must first help him become motivated so he can assume responsibility for making the changes needed to succeed. Helping a student gain willingness may be the greatest challenge for both of you. Once it is there, helping him gain the abilities needed should be comparatively easy.

In this endeavor, there are three aspects to motivation. First is an awareness that a problem exists. Second, there must be a desire for the problem to be eliminated. Third, there must be a willingness and commitment to put forth the time, effort, and energy necessary to eliminate it. If any of these three factors is missing, or even a little shaky, your chances of success are almost zero.

There is no parental exemption for this, because the role of helper is not a parental role. It's the role of a facilitator, coach, guide, and mentor. While doing these exercises, your own child must become your student. If the child isn't properly motivated, you cannot just insist that he comply with your instructions. You may be able to force a child to do what you want, but he won't gain any real benefit from it. It is very common, especially with younger children, that the parent is far more aware of the problem than the child. Your child cannot share your motivation. Each of you must have your own.

QUESTIONS TO ASK YOURSELF

So, if you are a parent, you should first consider your own motivation to be a helper.

Do you know that your child has a problem?

Would you like to help your child eliminate the problem?

Are you willing to put forth the time, effort, and energy to help your child eliminate the problem?

Are you willing for your child to become your student?

Are you willing to assume responsibility and control of the correction process?

When the time comes, will you be able to give your child control of correcting the problem?

If you can see your way clear to adopting this perspective, you have the green light to go forward. If the answer to even one of these questions is a little shaky, I recommend that you find someone else who is willing to do the instruction, or seek professional help. Contact a nearby Davis Facilitator. You can find them listed on the Internet at www.dyslexia.com or call the phone number in the back of this book.

BE OPEN AND HONEST WITH YOUR STUDENT

Over the years, while screening children for the Davis Dyslexia Correction Program, some parents asked me not to use the word "dyslexia" while talking to their children. These parents were attempting to protect their children from the emotional reality of their problems. They didn't want their children to suffer.

That was understandable, but in my opinion, it was the worst possible thing a parent could do to a child. These parents were providing their children with an inaccurate interpretation of reality. That can only serve to force a child into an inappropriate interpretation of his own existence. It also had the potential for sowing the seeds of additional emotional and psychological disorders in the future. Protecting a child in this way amounts to having the child practice insanity.

Eventually, the child will experience the truth, but by then his reaction won't be rational. These situations have always been heartbreakers for me, because it can be extremely difficult—sometimes impossible—to find a way to motivate students who have been subjected to this sort of denial. I had to refuse to work with some of these students and send them on their way with their learning disabilities unresolved. I could have helped if only the child had known my help was needed. But that would require that I openly discuss with the child his problem and his need for help.

The more aware a person is of having a problem,

the easier it will be to find a way to motivate him to solve it. The opposite is also true: If the person is unaware of having a problem, finding a way to motivate him may be impossible. It isn't difficult to find an entry, even in the most difficult cases, if you remember to follow these three steps:

1. Make sure the student recognizes that a problem exists.

2. Make sure the student desires to solve his problem.

3. Get the student's commitment to expend the time and effort necessary to fix the problem.

These are the three steps of motivation. Everyone is different, so each student's desire for change will vary, but every student will have some factors in common with others. To motivate anyone to do anything, we need to channel attention and energy in the direction we want it to go, and create an intention to get what we are able to give.

What to Say

1. Ask if there is a problem and get the student's agreement that one exists. Here, you will zero in on what the problem is from the student's perspective. You want to uncover some negative feeling about having this problem. It might not be perceived or expressed by the student as you would expect. It might appear as an indirect result of the learning disability observed by parents and teachers. Whatever it is, it must provoke the negative feeling of having the problem.

2. Ask the student if he would like to have that problem go away. In asking this question, you are actually asking the student to imagine not having the problem, and to imagine how that would feel. The difference in the *feeling* of having the problem versus not having it will create an emotion that will foster his motivation. Once that emotion is there, you can offer a solution.

3. Offer your help, and get the student's agreement to do what is needed to fix the problem. The student must agree to expend the time and effort required to eliminate the problem.

Here are some of the typical strategies we use when providing Davis programs professionally:

ADD AND ADHD MOTIVATION
These learning problems present a far greater challenge than reading, math, or handwriting problems. For one thing, the student is likely to be younger or less mature emotionally than students with the other problems. The very nature of ADD can inhibit the child's ability to perceive that a problem exists. If anything, he may see it as a problem that other people have with him, but not as his own problem.

So in searching for a way to motivate a child with ADD, you cannot focus directly on the condition itself. You must keep in mind that the concept of *consequence* probably isn't inherent to the child's thinking process, so the logic of cause and effect won't get you very far.

You need to find something the child wants but doesn't have. He won't yet understand that the ADD behavior is preventing him from getting it. Over the years, we have found that most ADD children are aware of one basic fact: *Other people don't like them.* Many think that even their own parents and siblings don't like them. They are highly aware that they have few, if any, real friends. We have found that most of them really want to have at least one friend. They want someone— anyone—to like them. So we often play on the desire for friendship, first to gain their cooperation, and then to build motivation.

Instead of asking, "Do you know you have a problem?" we ask, "Would you like someone to like you?" Or, "Would you like to have friends?" Occasionally, we go to the extreme of asking, "Do you want me to like you? Would you like me to be your friend?"

This strategy opens the door to saying, "I think I can help you with that. Would you like to try?" Once they say yes, you've got their cooperation to begin.

The *"Want someone to like you?"* motivation strategy won't work in every case. If it won't fly with the person you're working with, just use the strategy of finding *something* they truly want to achieve, dangle the carrot, and build the motivation from there. Once you place yourself in the position of being able to help them get what they want, you are in a position to help them get it.

MATH MOTIVATION

If a student isn't motivated to learn math, even the best technique of teaching it won't work. I'll tell you what I usually do, but you are more familiar with your student, so as always, adjust your language to suit the situation.

Helper: *I understand you have a problem with math. Is that right?*

Student: *I make a lot of mistakes. I don't get what the teacher means.* (This is an affirmative answer.)

Helper: *Would you like to learn how to do any kind of math problem so it will be easy?*

Student: *I've tried and I just can't do it.*

Helper: *Yes, but the question is, would you like to be able to do it?*

Student: *Yes, but it's too hard.* (This is an affirmative answer.)

Helper: *If we made it easy and simple to do, would you like to do it?*

Student: *Okay, but if it's too hard I'm going to quit.* (Affirmative answer. This is all the agreement you need.)

HANDWRITING MOTIVATION

These problems are so varied that the motivational strategies you use may require some discussion before you arrive at a "hot button" that accurately describes the student's problem. For example, can he accurately read back his own handwriting? Does that cause a problem with everyday tasks like taking notes in class or making a shopping list? Or does the student simply consider his penmanship unattractive? Does he get nervous trying to follow the teacher's penmanship instructions in school?

Once the discussion has brought the specific problem to the surface, ask the motivational questions. Here is an example:

Helper: *Do you know that [what was found in the discussion] is a problem?*

Student: *The teacher says it is.*

Helper: *So the teacher knows you have a problem. But do you know?*

Student: *Yeah, I can't do it very good.* (Affirmative answer.)

Helper: *Well, this book says I can help you by showing you a few tricks. It's different than the way they do it in school.*

Student: *How is it different?*

Helper: *We should be able to figure out what the real problem is and fix it. Do you want to try it?*

Student: *Okay.* (Affirmative answer.)

REINFORCEMENT

Whatever goal you start with, continue to put that same original goal in front of the student as you work your way through the correction procedures. Preface many of your statements with, "If you want [someone] to like you—" Or "To make math easy—" This will focus the student's attention on the following instruction. It keeps the goal alive and keeps the person going.

Once you have the student's commitment to try to fix the problem, the first and hardest step in the correction process is accomplished. It's time to solve the problem using the appropriate procedures.

CHAPTER 8

Perceptual Ability Assessment

Following is the assessment procedure as taught in Davis Orientation Mastery Workshops. It is designed to determine whether a person with a learning disability or other perceptual problem is a candidate for Orientation Counseling or Alignment. We use this assessment for children and for adults. We do not ordinarily make the assessment on children until the age of seven, because it is easier for younger children to understand and do the Alignment procedure.

The assessment is arranged in the form of a script, but there is no need to follow any rote procedure once you have a sense of what you are after.

Anyone who has the unique perceptual abilities of a picture thinker should be able to do this exercise easily. Pun intended, it should be a piece of cake for them.

However, if a person is obviously a nonverbal thinker, yet can't perceive a mental image as requested, use Alignment (Chapter 12). Stress, physical illness, and certain medications can also inhibit mental perception. If you suspect this is the case, you may want to contact a Davis Facilitator for assistance.

Davis Perceptual Ability Assessment

1. Greeting and Introduction:
Greet the person and introduce yourself. As appropriate, explain the nature of the assessment.

2. Concept clarification:

WHAT TO SAY:	WHAT TO DO:
Are you right-handed or left-handed?	*Make a note of the answer for future reference.*

What I am interested in is your imagination. Mainly that part of your mind where you can close your eyes and see the picture. Does that make sense to you?

If "yes," continue. If "no," explain further by asking her to imagine something she likes with her eyes closed. If the person can't form a mental (imaginary) image, stop.

Draw two circles on a blank piece of paper.

This circle represents you.

Point to one of the circles.

WHAT TO SAY:	WHAT TO DO:
This represents me.	*Point to the other circle.*
If you are looking at me, you are looking *from* here.	*Tap your pencil on the first circle.*
And you are looking *to* or *at* me over *here.*	*Draw an arrow from the first "you" circle to the second "me" circle.*
As long as we are looking with our eyes, we know exactly where we are looking from. But what about when we are looking at a picture with our minds?	*Point at your own eyes.* *Pause for a second.*
We are doing the same thing. We are looking *at* something— *from* someplace.	*Point at the "me" circle as you say "at." Point at the "you" circle as you say "from."*
I want to call the place we look from the MIND'S EYE because it is what sees when we are imagining. It is what is doing the looking.	*Make sure they get the idea.*

WHAT TO SAY:	WHAT TO DO:
Do you like cake?	*NOTE: Most people like cake, so in this example, we'll assume they do. If "no," try pie, pizza, or any distinctly shaped object the person can imagine easily.*
What kind of cake is the best kind?	*Note what kind of cake they like for future reference.*

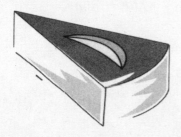

_____

_____

3. Assessment

Have the person sit directly in front of you, close enough that you could reach over and touch her forehead without getting out of your chair, but not so close as to make her feel uncomfortable.

WHAT TO SAY:	WHAT TO DO:

Is it all right if I touch your hand in what we are going to do?

Get her agreement.

We are going to use both your hands, so I need you to keep them available for me.

Take the person's opposite-to-handedness hand (if right-handed take her left hand; if left-handed take her right). Position the hand, palm up, about where she would hold a book while reading.

Let's imagine a piece of _____ cake is sitting right here in your hand. Tell me when you've got it.

"Imagine a piece of chocolate cake in your hand." (Tap the palm.)

"Close your eyes."

Describe the cake just as she described it, using her exact words: "A big slice of German Chocolate Cake," or "Angel Food Cake with green frosting."

WHAT TO SAY:	WHAT TO DO:

Close your eyes. I want you to keep your eyes closed until I tell you to open them. OK?

Make the request when she says she has a mental picture (if her eyes aren't already closed).

NOTE: If the person cannot visualize an object or has difficulty maintaining the image, you can either stop or attempt to coach the person in creating a mental image. Difficulty in visualizing indicates that Orientation Counseling is not appropriate. Use the Alignment procedure in Chapter 12 instead.

By asking simple questions, determine how the imaginary object is positioned in the hand. Continue until you also have a clear image of it sitting in the person's hand.

If you cannot make a visual copy of the imaginary object, at least get a sense of its size, shape, and position.

WHAT TO SAY:	WHAT TO DO:

I want you to shift your imagination and put your mind's eye here, where your finger is, and look at the piece of cake from *here*.

Take the index finger of the other hand between your thumb and middle finger. Raise the finger to a point a few inches from the handedness side of her forehead, on a level just slightly above eye level. The person's eyes should remain closed throughout the assessment.

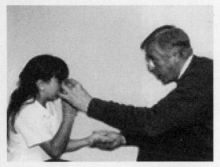

"Look at the piece of cake from here." (Tap the finger.)

Tap the tip of her index finger with your index finger as you say "here."

It's as if you raised up a little bit to get another view of the cake from *here*.

Tap the finger again. Wait several seconds . . .

Can you see the cake from *here?*

Tap the finger again.

WHAT TO SAY:	WHAT TO DO:

I want you to keep your mind's eye in your finger. Now I'm going to move your finger. I want your mind's eye to move with it, okay?

NOTE: If the person cannot make this first shift easily, do not continue. Go to step 4, ending the assessment. Explain that the assessment is over and that Orientation Counseling is not indicated. Use Alignment instead.

NOTE: Do not move the finger when giving instructions or talking to the subject. Make your statements before starting to move the finger and stop moving the finger before you begin talking again.

Move the finger slowly and smoothly to a position partway around the open hand. Keep the finger about the same distance from the open hand as the person's eyes are. What you are looking for is the ability to disorient or move the mind's eye.

WHAT TO SAY:	WHAT TO DO:

Can you see the piece of cake from here?

Tap the finger.

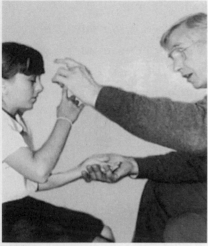

"Can you see the piece of cake from here?"

When "yes," ask questions that require a verbal response. Pay attention to response time, variation in speech pattern, and any manifestations of confusion or disorientation. Once you are satisfied that the person has actually shifted the mind's eye to the new position, you can go to step 4 and end the assessment at any time.

If you are not sure the person has actually moved the mind's eye, go to the next step.

I am going to move your finger again. I want your mind's eye to move with your finger. Okay?

Move the finger slowly and smoothly a little farther around the open hand. Don't move the finger more than a fourth of the distance around, above, or below the open hand during any one move.

Do you see the cake from here?

Tap the finger again.

WHAT TO SAY:	WHAT TO DO:
	When "yes" again, ask questions looking for indications that the person actually has moved the mind's eye. She should see a mental (imaginary) picture from the perspective of her fingertip, as if she were looking at the object from that position.
	Repeat the process of moving the mind's eye and questioning until you are satisfied the mind's eye has actually been moved.

4. Ending the assessment

I want to put your mind's eye back in the place where it was when we first started.	*Slowly and smoothly move the finger toward the eye on the handedness side of the person's body. When within a few inches of the eye, stop the finger.*
Take your mind's eye out of your finger and get your original view of the cake.	*Wait several seconds.*

WHAT TO SAY:	WHAT TO DO:
Do you have your original view?	*When "yes," move the finger in the direction of the lap and release the finger.*
Make the piece of cake go away, and tell me when it is gone.	*NOTE: If she has any difficulty making the object disappear, have her do a "reverse blink" by rapidly opening and shutting her eyes.*
	When it is gone, touch the palm of the open hand.
Put another piece of cake here in your hand and tell me when you have it.	*NOTE: The reason for forming a second image and making it disappear is to ensure the mind's eye has returned to its location. Moving the mind's eye has disoriented your student, so you want to reorient her now.*
Make this piece of cake go away and when it is gone, open your eyes.	*When her eyes open, move the open hand toward the lap and release it.*

CHAPTER 9

Orientation Counseling

The process of correction begins with getting the perceptual distortions under control. This means learning how to intentionally turn the disorientations on and off. Many of the symptoms of the students' problems are the symptoms of disorientation, so once the student knows how to turn the disorientations off, he can also turn the symptoms off. It may seem that the problem is solved, but orientation is merely the first step of the correction process.

It usually takes less than an hour to put someone through the initial Davis Orientation Counseling session. Working with students with "reading" dyslexia, the problem this procedure was originally designed for, the effect of Orientation Counseling is immediately seen. At the end of a successful session, with some help at catching disorientations as they occur, the student's reading skill is usually dramatically improved. It can appear that some kind of magic or miracle has just happened, but actually we are only seeing the person's real skills without the interference of disorientations. We have documented cases where the reading ability of teenagers has improved immediately by as many as eight grade levels as a result of Orientation Counseling alone.

It would be easy to believe something that could produce such a dramatic effect must be difficult to learn. In fact, it is very easy for nonverbal thinkers to learn. This is because they already know how to do it. They have been doing it since they were a few months old. They just were not consciously aware of what they were doing all along. Orientation Counseling enables them to understand a skill they already have and gives them a means to control it.

The procedure that follows may sound like a visualization exercise when you read it. Yet when properly applied, it can produce near miraculous results. There are only a few rules to follow.

1. Make sure the person is a candidate for Orientation Counseling by evaluating his ability to move the mind's eye with the assessment described in the last chapter.

2. Make sure the person wishes to perform the process. He must be willing and eager to do it. We generally do not perform this process on children younger than seven, because they haven't yet recognized disorientation as a problem at school. As far as they're concerned, nothing needs fixing.

3. Find a quiet, comfortable place where you won't be distracted by noises or interruptions.

4. Maintain a friendly, supportive control as you guide the person through the steps. He shouldn't have to think about what he's doing, but should simply follow the instructions.

5. Ensure the person is not tired, hungry, or taking any medications that might interfere with perception or thought.

What follows is a script of an initial Davis Orientation Counseling session as done at the Davis Correction Center. Correctly performed, it has produced a 97 percent success rate. If you don't get results, it's likely that one of the five rules listed above has not been followed.

Davis Orientation Counseling
Initial Session Procedure

1. Greeting and Introduction:
Greet the person and establish a rapport. As appropriate, explain the goal and objective of the procedure as stated at the beginning of this chapter.

2. Concept Clarification:
If you do not have the notes made during the assessment, you must establish the handedness of the person, and determine an object he can imagine easily.

Otherwise, use the same piece of cake or object that was used in the initial assessment.

Explain the concept of orientation as "putting yourself in the proper position in relation to the true facts and conditions of your surroundings."

Explain that disorientation is a condition in which the brain is not receiving what the eyes see or what the ears hear; the balance and movement sense is altered, and the time sense is either speeded up or slowed down.

WHAT TO SAY:	WHAT TO DO:
Before we start the session, I am going to go over everything we are going to do. I will show you on paper first, then we'll do it step-by-step. Okay?	*Get a piece of paper and have the person sit so the paper can be clearly seen.*

"I'll draw for you exactly what we're going to do so you'll know what to expect."

WHAT TO SAY:	**WHAT TO DO:**

There are two reasons why we are going over this first. One is to let you know what will be happening so there won't be any surprises. The other is to make sure you understand what I will be asking you to do.

Write the person's name, your name, the date, the name of the process, the object to be used in visualization, and the handedness of the person on the paper.

I do ask that you not do any of the process while I'm showing you on the paper. That would only create confusion. Just watch and listen. If you have a question, ask. After we finish going over it on the paper, I will walk you through it step-by-step. Okay?

Draw two circles on the paper. Make one circle a "top view" of a head. Make the other circle a "side view" of a head.

These are two views of the same head, looking down at it from the top and from the side.

WHAT TO SAY:	WHAT TO DO:

Like in the assessment, we'll have you imagine a piece of _____ in your hand.

Draw the object (the piece of cake used in the assessment) to be visualized in front of both views. On the side view the object should be below eye level at about a forty-five-degree angle from the line of sight.

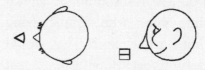

Then we will have you shift your imagination and put your mind's eye in your finger, off to the side and have you look at the piece of cake from *here*.

Put an X on the person's "handedness" side of the top view to indicate the position of the mind's eye (to the right if the person is right-handed).

Draw a straight line from the object through the top view. Extend the line well past the back of the head. On the side

WHAT TO SAY:	WHAT TO DO:

view, draw a straight line from the object, through the end of the nose, through the head, and extend the line well past the top back of the head.

Once your mind's eye is in your finger, we will have you imagine a line that goes from the piece of cake straight through your head. The line will go from the piece of cake into your nose, through your head, and will stick up about a foot or so above and behind your head.

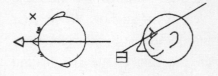

After you have drawn that line in, we will have you move your mind's eye around so it's a few inches above and behind your head and we'll have you position it on the line. Okay?

Make an X on each of the lines going through the heads.

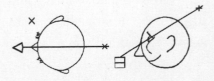

Do you know how an anchor for a boat works?

You have a heavy weight, and you attach a line or a chain to it. You attach the line to the boat and throw the anchor into

WHAT TO SAY:	WHAT TO DO:

the water. The anchor sinks into the mud or hooks on a rock or something and when the line is pulled tight it keeps the boat from moving. Right?

Be sure the concept of "anchor line" is understood.

We are going to use the same idea as an anchor. When your mind's eye is in the right place on the line above and behind your head, we are going to have you put an anchor line down to the top of each of your ears, and anchor it in. Then we'll have you put a third anchor line down to the top of your head and anchor it in there. Then we'll have you pull the three anchor lines and attach them together right where your mind's eye is.

Draw the three anchor lines on the paper as you explain it.

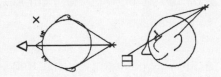

Any questions so far?

Once the three anchor lines are drawn in, we won't need the line that goes down to the piece of cake anymore, so you'll

WHAT TO SAY:	WHAT TO DO:

erase it out and it will be gone. We won't need the piece of cake anymore either, so we'll have you erase that out also.

To simulate erasing, draw a wavy line over one of the long lines and the object at its end.

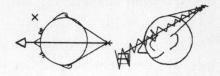

What you will have left are the three anchor lines that come together and make a point above and behind your head.

Draw three lines coming together, separately on another part of the paper. Draw a circle around the intersecting point.

We are going to call the place where the lines come together an ORIENTATION POINT. It is the PLACE where the lines end. We call the lines anchor lines, not to anchor the mind's eye there, which you can't do anyway, but to anchor this point there so it is in the same place all the time.

Any questions so far?

WHAT TO SAY:	WHAT TO DO:

What we are really after is a group of brain cells down in the middle of the brain that is responsible for disorientation. When those brain cells are turned off, our brain gets exactly what our eyes see, as our eyes are seeing it; and our brain gets exactly what our ears hear, as our ears are hearing it. Our balance and movement sense is accurate, and our sense of time is accurate. When those brain cells are turned on, the mind's eye has moved and we get disoriented. Our brain doesn't get what our eyes see; it gets what we think our eyes are seeing. Our brain doesn't get what our ears hear; it gets what we think our ears are hearing. Our balance and movement sense changes and our internal sense of time can either speed up or slow down. What we really need is the OFF SWITCH for those brain cells. That's what that orientation

WHAT TO SAY:	WHAT TO DO:

point is. It's the off switch for the disorientation.

The way we turn that switch off is simply by putting the mind's eye on that orientation point. That turns those brain cells off.

Draw an X inside the circle where the three separate lines come together.

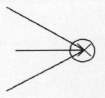

If our mind's eye is sitting in this spot, the brain cells are turned off. But if something happens that can cause a disorientation, the mind's eye doesn't stay there, it moves.

Draw three additional lines coming together, and put an X on the point.

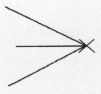

So it takes off, and we are disoriented. In the past, if we waited long enough, or if we

Draw an arrow from the point going off to the side.

WHAT TO SAY:	**WHAT TO DO:**

went for a walk, or did something other than what we were doing that caused the disorientation, eventually our mind's eye would come back, and we would be all right again—until something else caused another disorientation.

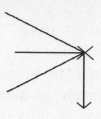

When we have an orientation point, we can deliberately bring the mind's eye back, put it on the point, and end the disorientation. We don't have to wait, or do something else, or torture ourselves. Simply putting the mind's eye back in that place turns off the disorientation. It also turns off the feeling of confusion and stops the mistakes.

Draw a line back to the point and retrace the X.

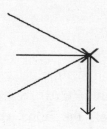

Any questions so far?

Draw three more lines that come together; they should be longer and bolder than the others.

WHAT TO SAY:	WHAT TO DO:

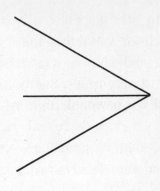

Of course, we can't see a mind's eye. In fact, it can't even see itself in a mirror. It is invisible. So we'll just imagine for a moment that this thing is a mind's eye. Okay?

When we get to the part of the session where you have put the three anchor lines in, your mind's eye will be sitting right where they come together.

Pick up some small object (a coin is fine) and hold the object where the person can see it.

For the first time in your life, you will have deliberately turned off the brain cells that cause disorientation. The only problem is we don't learn very much from doing something only once.

Position the object on the drawing, right where the three lines come together.

So when we have your mind's eye sitting on that point, we are going to find some real-life thing that will cause your mind's eye to jump off the point and disorient you.

Knock the object off the point where the lines come together.

WHAT TO SAY:	WHAT TO DO:

When that happens, I'll stop you from looking at the thing that made it jump, and have you simply put your mind's eye back on the point.

Put the object back on the point where the lines come together.

That will turn off the disorientation. The confusion will go away. Then I'll show you what made it happen.

Then we'll find another thing that will make it jump.

Knock the object off the point, and put it back again.

You'll put your mind's eye back, I'll show you what made it jump, and then we'll do it again. We'll do it again and again, until you are an expert at putting your mind's eye back on your orientation point. You will be able to do it quickly, easily, and know that you did it.

What you will have then is the ability to turn off a disorientation. It won't matter what turned it on; the action of

WHAT TO SAY:	WHAT TO DO:

simply putting your mind's eye on your orientation point will turn it off.

Any questions?

There is one more point we need to make.

We call this a line, because it has length to it. Just like this pen/pencil has length to it. But what about when we are looking down the length of it?	*Point to one of the anchor lines on the drawing.* *Pick up your pen or pencil.*
It doesn't look long at all, does it? It looks like a dot, doesn't it?	*Point the end of the pen or pencil toward the eyes of the person.*
If the mind's eye were sitting right here, it wouldn't see the three lines as lines at all, would it?	*Point to a place on the drawing where the three lines come together as you say "here."*
It would see them as three dots, or as one dot if they were pushed together. Do you agree?	*Draw one dot, and also three dots touching each other.*

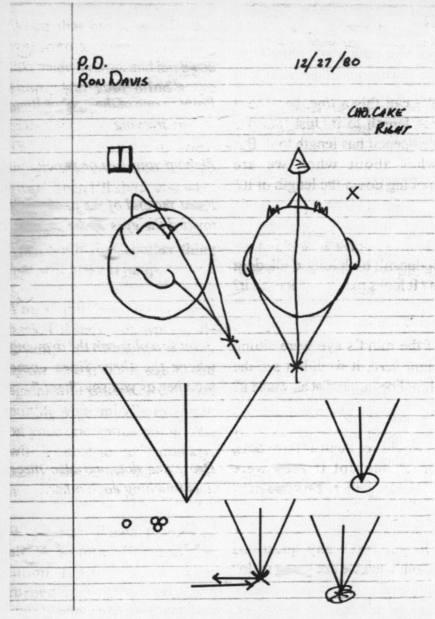

Your diagram for explaining a Davis Orientation Counseling
session will look something like this when you are finished.

WHAT TO SAY:	WHAT TO DO:

Do you have any questions about what we are going to do?

If you don't have any (more) questions, let's do it!

3. Process Sequence:

Is it all right if I touch your hands in what we're going to do?

Have the person sit directly in front of you, close enough that you could reach over and touch his forehead without getting out of your chair. Do not sit so close to the person that you make him feel uncomfortable.

Get consent.

We are going to use both of your hands, so I need you to keep them available for me.

Take the person's opposite-to-handedness hand (if right-handed take his left hand; if left-handed take his right). Position the hand, palm up, at the approximate place where a book would be held for reading.

Let's imagine a piece of _____ cake is sitting right here in your hand. Tell me when you've got it.

Describe the cake exactly as it was described to you in the assessment.

WHAT TO SAY:	WHAT TO DO:
Close your eyes. I want you to keep your eyes closed until I tell you to open them, okay?	*When you are certain he has formed a mental image, and the person's eyes are closed, take the index finger of the other (handedness) hand between your thumb and middle finger. Raise the finger to a point off to the side of the forehead on eye level (where you placed the X beside the head on the initial drawing).*
I want you to shift your imagination and put your mind's eye *here* . . . where your finger is, and look at the piece of cake from here.	*Tap the index finger with your index finger as you say "here."*
It's the same as if you leaned over and are looking from *here*.	*Tap the finger again. Wait several seconds.*
Can you see the piece of cake from *here*?	*Tap the finger. When "yes," go to the next step.*
Imagine a straight line that goes from the piece of cake into your nose, through your head, and sticks up about a foot	*Confirm that the line is there.*

WHAT TO SAY:	WHAT TO DO:

behind you. Draw that line in, and tell me when you have it there.

I am going to move your finger. I want your mind's eye to move with it, okay?

NOTE: Do not move the finger while giving instructions or talking to the person. Finish making your statement before starting to move the finger and stop moving the finger before you begin talking again.

I want to put your mind's eye on the line above and behind your head, so let me move your finger. Let your mind's eye move with it.

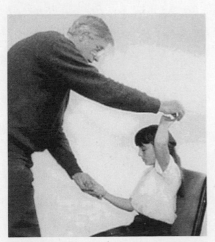

Stop the finger six to ten inches above and behind the head.

You will need to stand up to reach above and behind the person's head. Do so quietly and gently.

Move the finger s l o w l y and s m o o t h l y toward the midline of the body above and behind the head. Stop the finger about six to ten inches above and behind the head.

If the person's elbow is sticking out to the side of his

WHAT TO SAY:

WHAT TO DO:

body, you may need to turn his shoulder so the elbow points forward. This way the hand can easily reach behind the head.

I can't see the line. Only you can see it, so I need you to make the fine adjustment to get the mind's eye right on it.

Loosen your grip on the index finger, and allow the person to move the finger freely. It may take several seconds for the person to find the exact spot. When the person stops moving the finger, grasp it again.

Look to see that the finger is on what would be the midline of the body (it seldom is).

If it is on midline, go to the next step.

"I'll need you to make the final adjustment to get your mind's eye right on the line."

[It seems to be a bit off to the side. Is it all right if I move it just a bit?]

[If it is not on midline, without changing the distance from the head, move the finger to midline.]

WHAT TO SAY:	WHAT TO DO:

Pull the line to come to *here* and tell me when you've got it.

Tap the finger.

The person should now have an imaginary view from above and behind the head.

Tap the finger.

"Pull the line to here." (Move the finger to the midline and tap it.)

Can you see your ears from *here*? You can see right through your hair.

Tap the finger.

When "yes," go to the next step.

[If "no," have the person "feel" where the ears would be. If necessary, have him feel his ears with his hand (use the hand holding the imaginary object). If feeling them does not bring about seeing them, have

WHAT TO SAY:	**WHAT TO DO:**
	the person imagine where his ears would be and make a mental picture of them.]
Put anchor lines down to the top of each ear, anchor them in, and pull them to *here*.	*Tap the finger.*
Put another anchor line down to the top of your head, anchor it in, and pull it to *here*, as well.	*Tap the finger.*
Attach the three lines together.	*Confirm that this is done.*
I want to move your finger, but I don't want your mind's eye to come with it this time. Okay?	*Get agreement.*
As I move your finger, leave your mind's eye at the end of the lines.	*Move the finger to the side a few inches.*
Did your mind's eye stay on the lines?	*If "yes," move the finger over the shoulder in the direction of the lap. Release the finger and sit back down.*
[Take your mind's eye out of your finger and leave it on the lines when I move your finger.]	*[If "no," take the finger back to the position on the lines.]*

WHAT TO SAY:	WHAT TO DO:
	[Repeat this step until the mind's eye remains on the lines.]
We don't need the line that goes down to the piece of cake anymore, so erase it out and tell me when it is gone. We also don't need the piece of cake anymore, so erase it out and tell me when it is gone.	
What color are the three anchor lines you just put in?	*Make a note for your reference.*
	_____
Move your mind's eye to the place where the three (color) lines come together. Tell me when it is there.	
Do you see three dots, or one?	*Make a note.*
	_____

WHAT TO SAY: **WHAT TO DO:**

The anchor lines put in by the dyslexic during Davis Orientation Counseling will converge at a point six to ten inches above and behind the head. It will be at approximately a forty-five-degree angle, precisely on the midline of the body.

Are they the same color as the lines?

Make a note.

_____

What your mind's eye sees right now is what it should see when it is on the orientation point. Anytime you want to you can look with your mind's eye. If it sees what it sees right

At this point, the person should be able to get "on point" by mentally looking at the dots.

WHAT TO SAY:	WHAT TO DO:

now, you know it is on the orientation point.

If it doesn't see what it sees right now, you would know that it isn't on the orientation point and you would have to move it to the point to see what it sees now. Any questions?

If "no," go to the next step.

Open your eyes. Did it move when you opened your eyes?

[If "yes," tell her to put it back.]

[Put it back.]

[If "I don't know," have her close her eyes and check.]

[Close your eyes and look.]

4. Explanation:

I can't see your mind's eye. I can't see your anchor lines. If I hadn't been here while you were doing this, I wouldn't even know that you have them. If I can't tell, nobody else can tell either, so only you know for sure. You don't have to be concerned that anybody will think you are weird or that you

WHAT TO SAY:	WHAT TO DO:

are doing something that they can't do.

You can't touch a mind's eye; nothing can.

You don't have to worry about anything hitting it; or knocking it into a wall, a door, or anything else. You don't have to worry about catching it in the car door. It goes right through things, like they aren't even there.

Wave your hand above and behind your head.

When your mind's eye is sitting on the point, it is located by the lines that go to your ears and about the top of your head. You can't move fast enough to lose it. You can't turn your head fast enough to knock it off. It just sits there and goes where your head and ears go.

"You don't have to worry about knocking your mind's eye off or anyone seeing your lines."

Any questions?

WHAT TO SAY:	WHAT TO DO:
Do you know what the word *responsibility* means?	*Whether "yes" or "no," get the following concept across.*

Let me give you a (simple/simpler) definition. Responsibility is the ability and the willingness to control something. Control in its simplest form is the ability to cause something to change, or to cause it not to change.

Because I can reach over and move your hand, I am changing something about your body. That change is happening, and you're not doing it. I am responsible for that change. You aren't, because you didn't do it. Right?

Take one of the person's hands and move it a bit.

But I can't reach over and move your mind's eye. No one can. There isn't a person, animal, machine, or anything on this earth that can move your mind's eye one-billionth of an inch. But you can put it

WHAT TO SAY:	WHAT TO DO:

anywhere you want to. That means that you have total control, which also means that you have total responsibility for where your mind's eye is and what it does.

Do you agree?

That also means that when it jumps, when you get disoriented, you are the one that made it jump. When you were very young, you set it up so that whenever you were confused enough, your mind's eye would automatically go off and try to get rid of the confusion. When the confusion was about a real object it actually worked. It would get rid of the confusion. But it won't work with a symbol, and all words are symbols, so it won't work with words. Moving the mind's eye around just creates more confusion.

WHAT TO SAY:	WHAT TO DO:

Now you have a problem. Your mind's eye jumps every time you get confused, and you don't want it to do that anymore.

The problem is, it is still going to jump. If you try to hold it on the point to keep it from jumping, while at the same time you are automatically trying to make it jump, you are going to get a headache.

The only solution I know is to go ahead and let it jump. When it does, simply bring it back. That will be your job, your responsibility. Whenever it jumps, you put it back.

Do you have any questions?

Is your mind's eye still sitting on your orientation point?

[Put it back on the point.]

If "yes," go to the next step.

[If "no," have them put it back.]

WHAT TO SAY:	WHAT TO DO:

For the first little while after we get an orientation point, our mind's eye just floats around it.

It doesn't just sit there. This happens to everyone. We call it "drifting."

As soon as you get used to controlling your mind's eye, putting it and leaving it on the orientation point, the drifting will stop. Then when you put your mind's eye there it will just sit there.

Don't try to hold your mind's eye there, just let it drift. Every once in a while, move it back to the point and let go of it. If you try to hold it there you are just prolonging the drifting phase.

Any questions?

WHAT TO SAY:	WHAT TO DO:

5. Practicing Using Orientation:

Based on the disorientation history, select an activity, such as reading, which will disorient the person. Be alert for indications of disorientation. When a disorientation or mistake occurs, stop the activity.

If "no," continue the activity until it does.

Did your mind's eye move?

[If "I don't know," have her check.]

[Look with your mind's eye and see if it sees the (dot/ dots).]

When it has moved, have her put it back.

Put it back.

Then point out the stimulus that triggered the disorientation.

WHAT TO SAY:	WHAT TO DO:

Continue in this fashion until the person can quickly and easily put the mind's eye back on the orientation point, and sees that it makes a difference.

When the person can quickly and easily put the mind's eye on the orientation point, and knows that he has done so, the session is complete.

Point out each word that triggers a disorientation.

CHAPTER 10

Release and Review for Orientation Counseling

As dyslexics develop orientation skills, it will become obvious to them that if the mind's eye doesn't move, there are no mistakes. As they become more aware of their state of orientation, they will notice that whenever their mind's eye moves, they disorient. After they disorient, either they will make a reading mistake, or some "old solution" will automatically turn on.

It would seem that the next logical skill to develop would be a method of keeping the mind's eye on the orientation point. It is simple to do, and most students will try it. Unfortunately, this usually results in an intense headache.

The probable reason is that the mind's eye doesn't really move by itself. The student is, on a subconscious level, causing it to move. Moving it is an ingrained habit.

Learning about orientation and the benefits of not moving the mind's eye won't prevent the student from making this natural reaction to confusion.

So when the student becomes confused, he will be

attempting to move the mind's eye at the same time he is trying to prevent it from moving—literally working against himself. We call this holding. It creates tension, which results in the headache.

Simply telling students not to hold their mind's eye on the orientation point does not work. It's like telling them not to think about an elephant: It will cause them to do it instead of preventing it. The more they try not to hold, the stronger the holding will become.

Besides, there is no reason not to disorient when it's appropriate and useful.

Students who are holding the mind's eye rigidly on the orientation point will usually reach up and rub the back of the neck. When you see them do this, intervene with the Release procedure.

Signs of Holding

1. The student complains of a headache.

2. The student rubs or touches the back of the neck.

3. The skin tone becomes pale.

4. The brows wrinkle.

5. The student begins to look stressed or distressed.

Release Procedure

Have students go through the Release procedure by reading or reciting the following text to them. As you go, make sure they perform the action requested before doing the next step.

Make a loose fist—not too tight. Just let your fingers curl into your palm. Now think the thought "open hand," but instead of opening your hand, make the fist tighter.

Think the thought again, "open hand," and make the fist even tighter.

Again think the thought "open hand," and make the fist really tight—really, really tight, tight all the way up to your elbow.

Now without thought simply let your hand release. Let your entire hand go. Let your fingers find their natural place.

Feel the feeling that goes down your arm, through your hand all the way out to the tips of your fingers. That feeling is the feeling of release. When the word release is used, that feeling is what is meant.

The feeling of release is also the same feeling as the feeling of a sigh.

Do a sigh. Breathe in and hold it for a second or two. Then let the air rush out your mouth, with a "hunnnn" sound coming from your nose and throat.

A little sigh puts the feeling of release in your upper chest. A great big sigh can put that feeling all the way out to the tips of your fingers and toes.

Do a great big sigh. Get that feeling all through your body. Now let that feeling linger. Let that feeling remain in your body.

Now let your mind's eye have that feeling, by simply wanting it to. Your mind's eye can have that feeling. That's what your mind's eye should feel like.

Now have your mind's eye put that feeling down into your head and neck. You'll feel your neck muscles letting go. You'll feel them get loose.

If the student has a headache, use this step before continuing:
Now have your mind's eye put that feeling right inside the headache. Have your mind's eye fill up the headache with the feeling of release.
Have your mind's eye continue filling up the headache with release until it is completely gone.

In the future, whenever you have to put your mind's eye back on the orientation point, after you've got it there let it go. Turn it loose. It won't go anywhere, it'll just sit there. You don't have to hold it.

Every time you have to bring your mind's eye back, let it have that feeling of release. Then you won't have the headaches or the old solutions happening anymore.

End of process.

After the student has learned what release is and how to do it, there is no need to go through the whole procedure again. Simply ask or remind the student to "do release" whenever you notice him holding, concentrating, tensing up, or exerting a lot of effort.

Orientation Review Procedure

After a few hours, the orientation point established in the initial Orientation Counseling session may change location. As a result, from time to time you may need to check and see if it has moved, and if so, put it back to its original place. This is done with the Orientation Review procedure.

Simply ask students to put their finger *where their orientation point is*. Typically when I do it, I say: "Earlier when we did the orientation session, you got something called an orientation point. It's the place where the three lines make the point. Can you put your finger where that point is?"

The right place.

Her mind's eye is too low and off to the right.

When they do, check to see that their finger is on the midline of their body and between six and ten inches above and behind the head. If they put their finger in the right place, say: "That's good. Keep using that point and everything should be just fine."

If they put their finger anywhere other than in the right place, simply ask if you can do a "slight adjustment." (No one has ever said no.)

Grasp their finger between your thumb and middle finger, and gently pull it to the midline of the body. Tap the end of their finger with your index finger, and say: "Pull the point to here by adjusting the lines. Tell me when you've got it here." Tap the finger again.

When they tell you that the point is now where you want it, tell them: "That's good. Use this point, and everything should be just fine."

If the point continues to shift excessively, after doing the above adjustment, tell the student to "set the lines so they won't move."

"Adjust the point and lines to the midline."

Use Orientation Review only until you do the Fine-Tuning procedure covered in the next chapter. After doing Fine-Tuning, this method of checking the location of the orientation point is no longer appropriate.

CHAPTER 11

Fine-Tuning for Orientation Counseling

The Fine-Tuning procedure is a method for the oriented dyslexic to find his or her optimum orientation point. It is named for the process used to fine-tune a radio by moving the knob back and forth until the best possible reception is found.

The same thing can be done with the mind's eye. By moving it around the existing orientation point, the optimum place for orientation can be located.

There are several things to keep in mind here. The Fine-Tuning procedure is best done after the oriented dyslexic has had at least two days' experience at controlling orientation. Fine-Tuning should not be attempted until any and all drifting (slight floating of the mind's eye) has stopped.

During Fine-Tuning the mind's eye can move in every direction, not just back and forth. Also, at any time the mind's eye is moving, a person will feel out of balance. Fine-Tuning is done by moving it just a little, stopping it, and checking how things feel.

There are two ways students can tell when they have

reached their optimum orientation place. First, students will be perfectly balanced. They can stand on one foot without any movement in their foot, ankle, knee, hips, or torso. They can hold that position until their muscles become physically tired. At that point, they can still remain comfortably balanced by simply switching to the other foot. Secondly, when their mind's eye is at their optimum orientation place, students will experience a profound feeling of well-being—what I call the comfort zone. It will just "feel right."

Often while doing Fine-Tuning, students will move their mind's eye through the comfort zone. When this happens, the feeling of well-being will "wash" over them momentarily. They will probably smile and will look relieved. But if they don't stop their mind's eye at that exact location, the feeling will vanish as quickly as it occurred.

Assuming we start with the mind's eye above and behind the head, the observable phenomena of the relationship between the mind's eye and the body are:

1. If the mind's eye is left of midline, the body is out of balance to the left.

2. If the mind's eye is right of midline, the body is out of balance to the right.

3. If the mind's eye is too far back, even if on midline, the body is out of balance in the backward direction.

4. If the mind's eye is too far forward, even if on midline, the body is out of balance in the forward direction.

5. If the mind's eye is too low, the body is out of balance in the backward direction.

6. If the mind's eye is too high, the body is out of balance in the forward direction.

7. If the mind's eye is in front of the centerline of the body, (1) and (2) above reverse.

Using the above information, the student can find the optimum orientation point.

The student does the procedure by slowly moving and stopping the mind's eye within the general area of the existing orientation point. This is done until perfect balance is achieved, and he or she experiences an overall feeling of well-being.

Fine-Tuning Procedure

WHAT TO SAY:	WHAT TO DO:
	Explain the concept of fine-tuning a radio and how it can apply to finding optimum orientation.

WHAT TO SAY:	WHAT TO DO:

I want you to keep your eyes open during what we're about to do, okay?

Put your mind's eye on your orientation point.

"*Look at that picture up there.*"

Find a location where there is a view that extends a long way. This can be looking out of a window. Have the student stand facing the view.

Have the student check to see that the mind's eye is on the orientation point. Stand next to the student and point out a particular spot or point in the vista. The spot or point should not be below eye level.

WHAT TO SAY:	WHAT TO DO:

With your eyes looking at that (spot/point), balance on one foot.

NOTE: It does not matter which foot they balance on. They can switch feet if they wish.

Gently grasp the student by the shoulders, then release the grasp without moving your hands far from the shoulders.

"Keep looking at it and balance on one foot."

"Give it a push and see what happens."

Now push your mind's eye off your point in my direction, and see what it does to your balance. I won't let you fall.

If the student doesn't lean into you . . .

WHAT TO SAY:	WHAT TO DO:
[Give it a good push; I won't let you fall.]	*NOTE: It is important that the student feels the body go out of balance in the direction the mind's eye moves.*
Put your mind's eye back on point, and put your foot down.	
Tip your head forward, and look directly at the (spot/ point). Now balance on one foot.	*Locate another spot or point that is closer, about forty-five degrees below the line of sight. Direct the person's attention to the spot/point.*
Now, just like fine-tuning a radio, move your mind's eye around, and find the place where your body is in perfect balance.	

WHAT TO SAY:	WHAT TO DO:

"Look at that dime I threw on the floor and balance on one foot."

NOTE: This process takes as long as it takes. The student may not find optimum orientation on the first attempt.

Remember, while your mind's eye is moving, your balance is out, so move it just a bit, stop it, and then check. You'll know when you've got it by the feeling that it has.

Don't let them stop unless they are very close to, or have actually found, the optimum orientation place.

WHAT TO SAY:	WHAT TO DO:

Hold your mind's eye right where it is, and put your foot down.

When the student has found optimum orientation, or is getting tired and is very close, use the following steps to end the process.

Hold your mind's eye right where it is, and pull your (dot/dots) to where your mind's eye is. You're not moving the mind's eye; you're moving the point to the mind's eye.

Let your anchor lines set up and get hard right where they are, just like concrete sets up and gets hard. That way your point will be right where it should be and won't be moving around.

Confirm that this is done.

Explain that the student should use this procedure at least once a day to make sure the orientation point is optimum. Explain that, from time to time, the optimum place changes location for reasons unknown, and the student must adapt to that change using this procedure.

After Fine-Tuning, do not have the students try to put their finger where the point is. They probably won't be able to find it, and asking them to do so will only create confusion.

Future Orientation Review is done by simply having

students look down and balance on one foot, showing you that the balance is there.

There is only one optimum orientation point where all sensory data is most accurate. However, there are other orientation locations, one or more for each of the senses, where that sense will be very acute. The one for balance is two feet or more directly above the head, or forward of the center of gravity. When working with athletes, dancers, et. al. (anyone with excellent balance), make sure they are orienting above and behind the head and not directly above or in front of it. Having students look down while checking should ensure this.

CHAPTER 12

Alignment Procedure

If you have turned to this chapter, it means that your student is younger than seven years old, or you have determined he is primarily a kinesthetic or tactile learner, based on the Perceptual Ability Assessment exercise in Chapter 8.

Before you begin, your student needs an explanation of why you are giving him this tool. Tailor it to suit the student's age and needs. You must use words the student understands. Keep in mind that you are talking to someone who probably isn't very good at thinking with words. So keep the explanation as short and specific as possible.

In addition, the person you are talking to will probably have a very short attention span. If you talk longer than the attention span, you will lose them. Sometimes this can happen in as little as five to ten seconds. Any explanation you give will take longer than that, so here is a strategy to get beyond that limit: Simply break up the explanation into short pieces. Talk only for a few seconds, and then ask the student to respond in some way. A yes or no response is enough, and I suggest you mostly ask questions that require only a yes or no answer. Wait for a response before moving to the next question.

There isn't a set script to follow, so you will have to play it by ear. Here is an example of how I might explain the procedure to a seven-year-old child:

1. *What we're about to do is called* alignment. *Have you ever heard that word before?*

2. *For us, it's a name for a process that you can use to make sure that what your brain is seeing is what your eyes are seeing, and what your brain is hearing is what your ears are hearing. Let me hear you say the name—alignment.*

3. *It's really important, especially in school, that your brain is seeing and hearing what's really there. Because if it isn't the same, you will make a mistake. Do you know what a mistake is?*

4. *Now before we begin, you already have a natural alignment, it's a part of who and what you are. I know that because you can talk to me, and you wouldn't have been able to learn how to talk if you didn't. Say the word "gobbeldygook."*

5. *See, it's there. If it wasn't, you wouldn't have been able to say what I said. Are you with me so far?*

6. *But there is a problem. Sometimes your alignment gets broken or gets lost for a little while. And you don't even notice it. Have you ever caught it?*

7. *When that happens, your brain isn't going to see what's really there, and your brain isn't going to hear what's really there. And you can't tell, right?*

8. *This is a problem because it will make you make a mistake, and I don't think anybody likes to make mistakes. Do you like it when you make a mistake?*

9. *Do you think it would be good to have a way to tell if your alignment is there so you wouldn't make a mistake?*

10. *Do you think it would be good to have a way to fix it so if it isn't there, you wouldn't make a mistake?*

11. *Okay, what we can do is give you a new alignment. And this new alignment is one that you can check to see if it's there, so you can stop the mistakes. Would that be good?*

12. *Shall we do it?*

Only if the answer to the last question is *yes* would you continue. If the answer is *no*, either you have a motivation problem (see Chapter 7), or the student didn't really understand your explanation.

Alignment Orientation Procedure

Before you begin the Alignment procedure, you should first perform the Release procedure for Alignment. This is basically the same procedure used for Orientation Counseling in Chapter 9, but with the wording slightly simplified. The Release procedure and the Alignment procedure are given here in a script format so you can simply read it aloud to your student. Keep in mind that what you are doing is still in short segments, only now the responses you are looking for will be nonverbal.

RELEASE PROCEDURE FOR ALIGNMENT

1. *Get comfortable—as comfortable as you can.*

2. *Make a loose fist—not too tight. Just let your fingers curl into your palm.*

3. *Now think the thought "open hand," and make the fist tighter. Think the thought again, "open hand," and make the fist even tighter.*

4. *Again think the thought "open hand," and make the fist really tight—tight all the way up to your elbow.*

5. *Now without thought, simply let your hand go; let your fingers find their natural place.*

Note: The timing and pacing of the previous steps is important. Go slow enough that the student gets the effect, yet fast enough that he doesn't experience muscle fatigue.

6. *Feel the feeling that goes down your arm, through your hand, all the way out to the tips of your fingers. That feeling is the feeling of release. When the word "release" is used, that feeling is what is meant.*

7. *The feeling of release is the same feeling as the feeling of a sigh.* Demonstrate by doing an audible sigh.

8. *Do a sigh. Breathe in, hold it* (wait about three seconds), *now let the air rush out your mouth, with the "hunnnn" sound coming from your throat and chest.*

9. *A little sigh puts the feeling of release in your upper chest. A great big sigh can put that feeling all the way out to the tips of your fingers and toes. Do a great big sigh; get that feeling all through your body. Now let that feeling linger; let that feeling remain in your body.*

10. *Close your eyes. Feel your toes; find where your toes are and feel them from the inside.*

11. *Hold your feeling of your toes and feel your fingers. Find where your fingers are and feel them from the inside.*

12. *Now expand your feeling from your toes all the way to your ankles and from your fingers all the way to your wrists.*

13. *Now continue to expand your feeling from your toes all the way to your knees, and from your fingers all the way to your elbows.*

14. *Continue all the way to your hips and shoulders.*

15. *Now all through your body, all the way up to your neck.*

16. *Now all through your neck and head, all the way to the skin on top of your head. Get it all, including your ears.*

17. *Now do a great big sigh and flood your entire body with the feeling of release, all the way out to the tips of your fingers and toes.*

18. *Let that feeling of release remain in your body, and when it is comfortable to do so, allow your eyes to open.*

ALIGNMENT PROCEDURE

1. *Close your eyes again. The feeling of release should still be in your body.*

2. *Without moving your body, get the feeling that you are getting up. Get the feeling that you are getting up out of your chair.*

3. *Now get the feeling that you are moving around and standing behind the body that's sitting in the chair.*

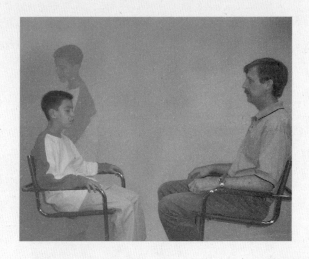

4. *Have the feeling that you are standing right behind the body that is sitting in the chair.*

5. *Reach out and put your imaginary hands on the shoulders of the body sitting in the chair.*

6. *Feel your shoulders with your imaginary hands, and feel your imaginary hands with your real shoulders.*

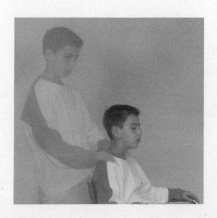

7. *Open your imaginary eyes and look down on the body sitting in the chair. You should see the top and back of the head.*

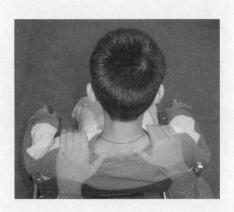

8. *Close your imaginary eyes, and keep the feeling of your imaginary hands on your shoulders.*

9. *Open your eyes. Keeping the feeling of the hands on the shoulders. Look around the room. Look at the things in relation to where your body is. See where the walls are in relation to your body.*

FINE-TUNING FOR ALIGNMENT

As soon as the student has done the Alignment procedure, you can go directly to the Fine-Tuning exercise. This is how he will check and adjust orientation in the future, whenever he feels the need.

1. *Now stand up, keeping the imaginary hands on your shoulders. Stand clear of the table and any chairs.*

2. *Balance on one foot. Let the imaginary hands hold you in balance. If you feel out of balance in any direction, move the imaginary body slightly in the opposite direction until you feel in perfect balance.*

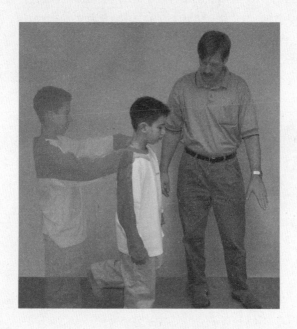

3. *When you have found your perfect balance, lock your imaginary elbows, so the imaginary body will always be in the same position when the imaginary hands are on your shoulders.*

4. *Now you can walk around, keeping the imaginary hands on your shoulders.*

5. *Anytime you want to or need to, you can realign by getting the feeling of having your imaginary hands on your shoulders.*

At this point, your student should be able to reorient whenever it's needed. At the beginning, you may want to remind him periodically while you are going through the correction exercises. Whenever a mistake occurs or you see signs of disorientation, just ask a question like, "How is your alignment?" Or simply say, "Check your alignment; feel your imaginary hands on your shoulders."

CHAPTER 13

Energy Dial Setting

This procedure was originally developed for people with ADHD, the "hyper" form of ADD. We now recommend it for anyone using any of the processes in this book, because it can also enhance performance in math, handwriting, athletics, and social skills.

Dial Setting gives your student a means of adjusting his experience of time and his energy level so they are appropriate for a given situation. What we are doing is installing an imaginary energy level control the person can check and adjust if need be. A parent can do it with a child, or an adult can do it instructed by a friend acting as a helper. You can do it anytime after Fine-Tuning for Orientation or Alignment is complete.

A dial, according to the dictionary, is *a circle around, or on which, a scale is marked, so that the position of a pointer, rotating about the center of the circle, can be stated.* A dial does two things:

- It shows the operating condition of something. The knob on a stove tells you how hot a burner could be; the volume control on a stereo tells you how loud the sound is, or will be when you turn it on.

- It also allows you to change the operating condition. You can turn the stove burner up and down or adjust the volume of the stereo with the dial knob.

The dial you will give your student will help him control the rate at which he experiences change (time or speed) and the energy level he experiences. It is set in place using imagination and feeling, or physical sensation.

Why a Dial?

Disorientation causes distortions in perception and variations in brain chemistry. The brain chemistry fluctuations explain many of the symptoms and characteristics of attention deficit disorder, including hyperactivity and hypoactivity.

With orientation, perception is corrected, and that has a stabilizing effect on brain chemistry. However, changes in brain chemistry are much like the swings of a pendulum. It takes time for them to even out and become stable. Because the brain was functioning with different levels of chemicals for so long, once things even out, the levels may be higher or lower than the norm. The dial is a tool the student can use to make the adjustments to the apparent norm in less than a minute.

A FACILITATOR'S REPORT

The following is an example of how effective Dial Setting can be for ADD students when properly applied. This is an actual clinical case study from Paula Morehead, a Davis Facilitator at the Dyslexia Center of the South in Birmingham, Alabama.

"I talked to the father of a thirteen-year-old boy who was interested in the Davis Dyslexia Correction program for his son. During the conversation, I learned that the boy had been taking Ritalin for the last six years. After such a long period on the medication, his son could hardly sit still even for a little while unless he was taking the medicine. I recommended that he talk with his son's doctor and see about taking him off the medicine at least two weeks before the scheduled program. He agreed to do this.

"When they arrived to begin the five-day program, the child was having a very difficult time sitting still for any part of the initial consultation. We made it through, and I was able to establish that he really wanted to be able to read and he wanted to stop taking the medicine. He said it was embarrassing to have to go to the health room every day and take medicine like a baby.

"As soon as we completed the initial Orientation Counseling session, I introduced Dial Setting to him. We talked for a long time about the different kinds of dials there are and their uses. We then established a dial for him to use to control his energy instead of having to take medicine to do it. I must admit, by the end of the first day, I wasn't sure what would happen. I was tired from watching him bounce around in his seat.

"The next day was a little better. He had started reading on Monday at a first-grade level, but we had to go to a place where there was nothing in his line of vision. If he could see anything distracting, he could not stay oriented because 'things moved around the room' and he wanted to watch them.

"On Wednesday, after Fine-Tuning, he was a completely different child. I pulled out *Charlotte's Web* and he read the first two pages with only two or three mistakes. I asked him about the things around him and he said, 'Wow, now I can read and the things in the room don't move around anymore.' He finished the book by Friday morning.

"In the post-assessment reading inventory, his reading level increased from the first-grade level to a fifth-grade level. He was really excited and was ready to go back to school in the fall. When I heard from him four months later, he told me he was still doing fine without medication."

The Dial Setting Procedure

Ask: *"Can you tell me what a dial is?"*

If the student doesn't know, explain it fully. You may even experiment with some various dials and talk about what they do at different settings. Make sure the person understands what a dial looks like, and that it both shows the level of function and controls the level of function.

Explain that you will have the student imagine a dial that shows his energy level and the rate at which he experiences time. Tell the student they will be the same. If necessary, explain what you mean by energy level.

Say: *"Imagine a dial that shows your energy level."*

Once the student complies, ask him to describe it. Ask enough questions to make sure there is a reasonably vivid mental picture. What color is it? How big? How is it shaped? If it doesn't have ten gradations or levels on it, then tell the student to change the image of the dial so it has ten different numbers or setting point.

Say: *"Position the dial somewhere in front of you to the left or right side—not right in front of you.*

When he has complied, say, *"Put your hand in the space where the image of the dial is."*

Ask: *"If the dial shows your energy level right now, what is the setting of the dial?"*

If the dial is set at five or below say: *"Set the dial up to eight. Do you feel the surge of energy? Do you feel the air around you getting cooler? Do you notice the feeling of being more awake? Do you feel jittery at this level?"*

If the dial is set above five say: *"Set the dial down to three. Do you feel yourself slowing down? Do you feel the calm feeling? Do you feel the warm feeling? Do you feel the relaxing feeling?"*

You might want to ask other questions about what the student is feeling. You want to draw his attention to whatever changes took place. Don't comment on the answers as being correct or not. The student will experience whatever he experiences.

Once the student notices some differences, ask him to set the dial in the opposite direction (if it was moved to three, go to eight, if it was moved to eight, go to three). Then ask the appropriate questions from above.

After the student describes the changes, ask him to set the dial back to its original setting and notice the changes. The changes will be more subtle, because the difference is less. But by now, he should be able to notice the difference easily.

Now it's time to introduce the idea of appropriate dial settings for different activities. You could ask:

"What would be the best dial setting when you're playing sports?"

"What would be the best dial setting for watching TV?"

"What would be the best dial setting when you're in class listening to the teacher?"

"What would be the best dial setting for brushing your teeth?"

"What would be the best dial setting when you're doing homework?"

It is too soon for him to really know the answers, but you should have him thinking in the right direction.

End this activity by telling him, *"Your dial is your tool—it belongs to you now. You can use it however you want. I suggest you try it out—experiment with it— try different setting for the different activities. You get to decide what works best for you."*

Important Note: After the Energy Dial is installed, and the student has had a chance to use it on his own, you should not tell your student where to set it. He created the dial, he owns it, and he is in control of it. If you told him to turn it up or down, you would be depriving him of responsibility and self-control. For a while, you might want to remind him to check by asking questions like these:

"Have you checked your dial lately?"

"Where is your dial set?"

"Is that level appropriate for what is happening right now?"

Pretty soon, the student will start making the necessary adjustments automatically.

FOLLOW-UP

Go for a walk where there are a lot of people to observe. Point out a particular person and ask, "If that person had a dial, what would it be set at?" Continue asking about other people's dial settings until the student can quickly tell you what it would be. Don't be surprised if the student says that other people's dials are set lower than you think they are, especially if you are working with someone who has ADHD. For a hyperactive person, you should present a simple truth that goes something like this:

"Other people will be able to communicate and get along with you better if you set your dial the same as theirs. That way, you're operating on the same wavelength."

Keep in mind that the effect of changing dial settings will be more dramatic with a child than an adult. It seems that the older we get, the smaller the range we can produce. What was my own setting of six twenty years ago is now my setting of ten at age sixty. I also experience the most dramatic sensations when setting my dial from three to one.

Over the years, there have been only a few adults

who attended my workshops who couldn't get a dial to work for them at all, or the changes in the settings produced so little sensation that they couldn't verify the effect. I suspect that was because they were skeptical to begin with, and so missed out on a great tool. For the rest of us it would work just fine.

CHAPTER 14

Coordination Therapy

After the Fine-Tuning process is completed, there is a fast and simple way to put an end to *left/right confusion* problems for good. This process also addresses the dyspraxia problem described in Chapters 17 and 24. We call it Koosh Ball Therapy because we use the light, furry toy balls made of rubber band material for the process. We don't recommend other balls like tennis balls or Ping-Pong balls, because they have a tendency to bounce out of the person's hands before they're able to grasp them. If you can't find Koosh Balls at a local toy store, you can make do with a pair of rolled-up socks or beanbags.

You can start doing this periodically after Fine-Tuning, described in Chapters 11 and 12.

Stand six to ten feet away from the person (closer for small children). Start by telling the student to "check your point" if you used the Orientation Counseling procedure, or "check your imaginary hands" if you used Alignment. When the person is oriented, have them balance on one foot. They can stand on either foot, and can switch feet at any time.

Hold both balls in one hand. With the student comfortably balanced on one foot, say "Catch one ball in one hand and the other ball in the other hand."

1. Underhanded, toss each ball one at a time. Toss gently, aiming about chest high. Each time you toss a ball, say "One in one hand, one in the other."

2. When the student can easily catch a ball in either hand without losing balance, repeat, "One in one hand, one in the other." Then toss both balls *simultaneously.* Aim for a position directly in front of the person on the midline of the body. If properly tossed, one ball will be on each side of the midline.

"One in one hand, one in the other."

Be sure to toss them so they can be easily caught. When the student catches both balls, praise the student and do it again.

3. After a while, say, "I am going to toss them both to one side of you. I want you to catch them without losing your balance." Do this for each side so the student has to cross the midline with the other hand to catch one of the balls. Don't aim too far to the side, or you will cause the person to lose balance.

Crossing the midline.

CHAPTER 15

Symbol Mastery and Concept Mastery

To understand the strategy of Symbol Mastery, we need to consider two factors:

First is the premise that language mirrors the thought process. If it didn't, language would probably be too complicated for anyone to learn. All languages are composed of symbols, and all symbols have three aspects:

- What the symbol sounds like when we hear it.

- What the symbol looks like when we see it.

- What the symbol means.

Second is the observation that there are two basic methods of human thought—*verbal conceptualization* (thinking with sounds) and *nonverbal conceptualization* (thinking with pictures).

When a person uses verbal conceptualization, he is thinking with the sounds of the symbols. When a person uses nonverbal conceptualization, he is thinking with mental images. Two of the three components of a symbol can be conceived as mental images—what it looks like when we see it, and what it means or stands for. When using nonverbal conceptualization, the individual obviously isn't thinking with how the symbols look: If he were, he would have to read his thoughts like a newspaper. So what's left? A person thinking in the nonverbal mode is actually thinking with the *meaning* of the language in the form of mental pictures of the concepts and ideas it contains.

Nonverbal thought doesn't require literacy. An illiterate person can communicate without knowing what the symbols look like. They are important only for reading, writing, math, music, and other forms of stored data. Literacy, then, is established as the person learns how the symbols look and becomes able to recognize them as representing certain things or concepts.

Mastery and Automaticity

When we master some skill like riding a bicycle or driving a car, we incorporate the process of doing it into our identity. With some practice, we can perform the activity without conscious thought. The ability has become a part of who and what we are. When we master a word or concept, it also becomes a part of who and what we are. In order to accomplish this, two things must be involved—the personal experience of the individual and the creativity of the individual.

Symbol Mastery is performed by having a person personally experience the creation of a symbol. The student creates all three parts of the symbol in the same place, at the same time.

For reading dyslexia, we start by having the student master the basic symbols—alphabet letters, punctuation marks, and on some occasions numerals. Depending on your student's problems you can determine whether or not mastering these basic symbols would be appropriate.

MATERIALS NEEDED

- 2 pounds of plasteline clay

- a plastic knife for cutting clay

- a dictionary with clear, simple definitions

- other reference material as needed if you are working with technical terms

- paper towels for wiping clay off hands and surfaces

- for Alphabet Mastery, make enlarged photocopied letter strips from the pages at the end of this chapter

BASIC RULES FOR THE HELPER

- Be alert for any and all disorientations.

- Check orientation/alignment after each disorientation and after breaks.

- Be patient, polite, kind, inquisitive, and observant.

208 The Gift of Learning

- Refrain from touching your student's clay models. If you don't clearly see what is being represented, simply tell the student that you can't see that part of it, and discuss that part of the meaning if necessary.

For the process to be fully effective, the models made must be entirely the student's own creation. As a helper, you are there to provide encouragement, not criticism. Asking questions is the best way to help your student formulate ideas and challenge his imagination. The student's models only need to clearly show the meaning. This has nothing to do with sculptural artistry.

Symbol Mastery of Letters, Punctuation Marks, and Numerals

ALPHABET MASTERY PROCEDURE

The purpose of mastering the alphabet is to find and eliminate any letters that may be triggers for disorientation. This procedure can take anywhere from a few hours to two days.

1. Familiarize students with clay. Shaping. Cutting. Rolling.

2. At any sign of disorientation, always stop and politely ask the student: "check your orientation alignment," or "get your dot/dots." Then resume.

3. Have the student make the uppercase alphabet letters, A to Z, in forward order. Letters should be at least two inches high. Make an example letter strip by following the instructions at the end of this chapter, and keep it nearby for the student to look at.

4. Ask the student, "Whose alphabet is this?" Repeat the question conversationally until the student says, "It's mine." Then ask the student, "Why?" or "How come?" until the student says, "Because I made it," or "Because I created it."

5. Ask the student, "Are you satisfied with your alphabet?" If not, ask what could be better, and have them correct it until they are satisfied with it.

6. Ask the student how many letters are in the alphabet. If unsure, have the student count them (slowly). Repeat this activity until the student is absolutely certain there are twenty-six.

7. Have the student slowly and deliberately touch and say the name of each letter in forward order, from left to right.

8. As appropriate, have the student check to see all the letters are correctly positioned and sequenced, and similar in size. Let the student find the errors by comparing with the examples.

9. Have the student touch and say the name of each letter in backward order, starting from Z.

10. Note any errors, hesitations, and confusions. On letters that cause signs of disorientation:

> **A.** Ask for words or names that begin with that letter. (Optionally, ask for associations or reminders.)
>
> **B.** Ask the student to pick up the letter, place it in the palm of one hand, cover it with the other, get on point or aligned, and then reveal the letter to see if it is still triggering disorientation. Repeat this as needed until the letter no longer triggers disorientation or feels "hot."

11. On two letters that cause confusion or get mixed up, ask the student:

> **A.** "Tell me something similar about these two letters."
>
> **B.** "Tell me something different about these two letters."

Alternate asking (A) and (B) until there are no more answers.

For sequential errors or omissions, ask, with student looking at the letter:

> **A.** "What letter comes before_____?"
>
> **B.** "What letter comes after_____?"

12. Have the student touch and say the letters forward and backward until it becomes easy and comfortable, without hesitations.

13. Have the student say the alphabet forward and backward, looking at the letters, without touching them.

14. Call out a letter of the alphabet, and have the student touch and say what letter comes before and after that letter. Do this until the student can easily and quickly find any letter in the alphabet.

15. Have the student say the alphabet backward, taking as many "peeks" as needed to get through it. Again, look for letters that cause problems, repeated looks, and repeated confusions. Check for orientation/alignment, and apply steps (10) or (11) above to these letters as needed. Do this until the student can say the whole alphabet backward at least once without looking.

16. If any signs of struggling or frustration appear, *BACK OFF* from this task. Take a short break. Then check orientation/alignment and go back to the step just preceding the one where trouble occurred. Repeat that step to a new success.

17. Continue to practice the alphabet backward and forward until the student knows it and can easily and comfortably recite it in both directions. Praise lavishly when this is accomplished. Always take a good break after this accomplishment.

18. Have the student make the alphabet in lowercase manuscript backward, z through a, in reverse order (but not with reversed letters). Make an example

Your student will learn the alphabet both forward and backward.

letter strip by following the instructions at the end of this chapter, and keep it nearby for the student to reference.

19. As above, monitor for problem letters, check orientation/alignment as needed, and have the student check for accuracy.

20. Repeat steps 4–17 on the lowercase alphabet.

21. Do some fun practical exercises like naming letters in the environment, or finding letter sections in a dictionary or phone book.

*This is how we have students master
punctuation marks in clay.*

PUNCTUATION MASTERY

1. Go over the definition of "punctuation": marks used in writing and printing to help make the meaning clear.

2. Beginning with the period, have the student make the period with clay.

3. Have the student write or copy the name of the mark on a piece of paper; half a sheet of regular typing or copy paper works well.

Marks to model:

period   .

question mark   ?

exclamation mark   !

comma	,
semicolon	;
colon	:
hyphen	-
dash	—
parenthesis (plural: parentheses)	( )
brackets	[ ]
quotation marks	" "
virgule or slash	and/or
ellipsis	. . .
apostrophe	it's

4. Point out the placement of the mark in relation to words, and have the student place the clay model of the mark on the paper in the correct relationship to what they have written.

5. Ask, "Whose is this?" and "How come?" as done with the alphabet letters.

6. Have the student touch and say the name of the mark.

7. Explain what the student should *do* when he or she sees the mark while reading aloud. Stop for periods, pause for commas, lilt the voice for question marks, etc.

8. Repeat steps 2–7 for all the punctuation marks.

9. Referring to a grammar book or dictionary, go over the common usages of any mark that the student does not understand.

10. Have the student find examples of each mark in various texts such as a primer, magazine, sign, etc. Also point out how each shape differs depending upon print style or typeface.

NUMERALS MASTERY

Ask the student to form the numerals zero through ten, about two inches in length, on the tabletop. Then put the correct number of clay balls in a column above each numeral. Ask the student to put the spelled form of the word underneath each numeral.

Have the student point to the balls and say, "*This is* (number), *meaning* (count the balls)."

Have the student point to the numeral and say, "*This says* (number), *and means* (count the balls)."

Have the student point to the word and say, "*This says* (number), *and means* (count the balls)."

This and other math exercises are covered in Chapter 19, "Twelve Exercises for Teaching Math."

Symbol Mastery for Words

Now that the student has mastered the basic elements, it is time to move on to words.

EXERCISE ONE: CREATE A NEW WORD

Start with this simple exercise to establish the idea that a word has three components: (1) what it looks like, (2) what it sounds like, and (3) what it means.

These are the instructions to give your student:

1. Make something in clay that is totally his own invention or fantasy. It could be a machine, an idea, an action, a description, a strange animal that doesn't exist, or anything (the concept). When complete go to the next step.

2. "Tell me about what you made." When the student is finished describing the creation, tell the student, "What you just told me is the 'meaning' of what you created."

3. "Give your creation a made-up name."

4. "Make that name in clay with the letters of the English alphabet. You can spell it any way you like" (the written symbol).

5. "Tell the model its name and what it means. You are (name), and you (are—mean—do)".

6. Tell the word what it "says" and how it is spelled." You say *(name). (s p e l l)*.

Next, discuss the evolution and purpose of words with a dialog something like this:

"You just created a new word—a sound symbol and a written symbol that means the thing you first made in clay. You have mastered it, because you created it, and you know what it means, what it sounds like, and what it's supposed to look like.

"Of course, you're the only one who knows what your word means and how to say it properly, and how it's supposed to be spelled. Now, what if you wanted to teach that word to someone else? Just saying it to them or showing them the written word wouldn't be enough, would it? For them to really understand it, they would need to know what the letters and sounds you use are supposed to mean or represent, right?

"Every language is composed of words that somebody made up. They started with an idea or image that was in their mind, made a sound for it, and then created symbols that represented that sound. When a lot of people learned the word and agreed that that sound and those symbols would always mean the same thing, they could use that word to communicate in speech and in writing.

"In English, we have thousands of words that already have sounds, and letters everybody has agreed upon. Their meanings and sounds are described in the dictionary. With Symbol Mastery, you get to create for yourself what those words mean, what they sound like,

and what they look like. After you do this with words that were hard for you to spell, read, write, or understand, you will know and understand them in the same way you know and understand the word you just created."

EXERCISE TWO: SYMBOL MASTERY PROCEDURE FOR WORDS

To get familiar with the steps of Symbol Mastery, do this exercise with some easy words that only have one or two definitions. Pick a word that is the name of something real (a noun) such as *dog, cat,* or *umbrella.*

Instruct your student in following the nine steps of the Symbol Mastery process:

1. *Look up the word.*
(In a dictionary, glossary, or other reference book.)

2. *Pronounce the word.*
(If your student isn't familiar with the pronunciation key, pronounce the word for him and have him repeat it.)

3. *Read one definition and its example sentences aloud.*
(If your student isn't capable of reading the definition, read it to him.)

4. *Establish a clear understanding of the definition.*
(Discuss it with your student. Take turns making up sentences or phrases using the word with that definition. Do this until your student can mentally picture this definition.)

One student's model of the word and.

5. *Make a clay model of the concept described by the definition.*

6. *Make the word with clay.*
(Be sure the spelling is correct. Make lowercase letters unless the word normally begins with capital letters.)

7. *Say aloud to the model of the concept:*
"This is [*word*] meaning [*definition*]."
(Example: "This is [*tall*] meaning [*of more than normal height*]."

8. Say aloud to the model of the word:
"This says [*word*]."
(Example: "This says [*tall*].")

9. *Make a mental picture of what has been created.*

Additional Exercises (optional)

A. Touch and say the letters of the word.
B. Spell the word backward and forward.
C. Write the word.
D. Make up more sentences and phrases until the student can do so easily. Be sure the usage of the word matches the definition the student just made.

Now repeat the exercise with a common verb and adjective. You will be using this procedure to help your student master various terms as part of the correction procedures that follow. It is an effective way for students to learn basic vocabulary words, as well as the key terms of any subject.

Other Uses

Symbol Mastery isn't just limited to words. You can use it to master any kind of symbol, such as those for math, music, or chemistry. When studying a subject, it is a good idea to master any new, unfamiliar terms listed in the textbook glossary.

Concept Mastery

Concept Mastery is done in the same nine-step sequence as Symbol Mastery, but with one major variation. The clay scenario depiction of the meaning must include a model of *self*. The clay model must show how the person is, or could be, involved in the concept he is modeling. So the first step of Concept Mastery is to have your student make a clay model that represents himself.

This can be a bit tricky. If you simply tell someone to make a clay model of himself the clay model would show only the physical characteristics. We aren't interested in those; we are interested in the person's *identity*. The identity of the person cannot be seen, so it isn't even necessary to make the model look like the student. The model *represents* self rather than means self. It only needs to be a human figure. The oral part of the process is where the significance is inserted. The language you use will need to be adjusted to identify the model as representing the identity of the student.

When you instruct your student to make the model, your words must convey the idea that the model only represents the person, and isn't a definition of the person. For example:

- Say: *"Take some clay and make a model of a person. The person is going to be you, and you will be using the model to show how you fit into the world of ideas. The model will represent who you are. The model should be about two or three inches tall, and should be able to stand up on its own."*

- As the student is making the model, casually ask: *"When you are talking to someone, what word do you use to identify yourself?"* You are looking for the answer "Me," or "I."

- If the student doesn't understand this question, point out something that belongs to the student, like his shoe, and ask, *"Who does that [shoe] belong to?"* When the student answers *"Me,"* say, *"That is what we will name your model."*

- When the model is completed, say, *"Make the word* **'me'** *out of clay and put it below the model."*

- When done, say, *"Point to the model of the person and say, 'This represents me.' When you say the word 'me' touch yourself on the chest with your other hand."* Have the student do this.

- When done, say, *"Point to the <u>model</u> and say, 'This represents every experience me' (touch your chest) 'has ever had.'"* Continue by saying, *"All of the knowledge, all of the wisdom, and all of the understanding."* Have the student do this.

- When done, say, *"Point to the <u>word</u> and say, 'This represents me.' When you say the word 'me' touch yourself on the chest with your other hand."* Have the student do this.

- When done, say, *"Point to the word and say, 'This represents every experience me' (touch your chest) 'has ever had.'"* Continue by saying, *"All of the knowledge, all of the wisdom, and all of the understanding."* Have the student do this.

When this is finished the student can remove the word, but will keep the model for future use.

BASIC CONCEPTS

The basic concepts below are those we have found to be missing or inaccurate in most students with learning disabilities, particularly if they have ADD or acalculia. They should be done in the sequence presented here. The meaning of the concepts are provided so you and your student don't need a dictionary or reference book.

The illustrations below show two examples of students' models for the concepts "change" and "time." They are for example purposes only, not for copying. Your student should create his own basic concepts from scratch, using the descriptions of the concepts below and his imagination. Of course, you will want to discuss the concepts in detail, and possibly point out real world examples.

Here are a few tips:

- It may be necessary to make more than one model of self for a scenario to show these concepts.

- In most cases, it is best to limit the number of concept words mastered to just a few per day.

- Make sure the student's clay figures and models are three-dimensional, representing physical reality in a recognizable way and not overly abstract. A chunk of clay cannot be representative of a car; the chunk should at least have four wheels.

- Use clay arrows to show directions or sequence.

- To show that something is an idea, make a clay rope into a "cartoon bubble" that is attached to the clay person's head, and make the "idea" inside the cartoon bubble.

The basic concepts your students should master are:

1. self: *a model of self, representing all the knowledge, wisdom, and understanding of the person's lifetime, described earlier.*

2. change: *something becoming something else.*

3. consequence: *something that happens as a result of something else.*

4. cause: *something that makes something else happen.*

5. effect: *something that happened as a result of something else.*

6. before: *happening earlier.*

7. after: *happening later.*

8. time: *the measurement of change in relation to a standard.*

9. sequence: *the way things follow each other one after another in size, amount, time, arbitrary order, and importance.*

10. order: *things in their proper places, proper positions, and proper conditions.*

11. disorder: *things not in their proper places, and/ or not in their proper positions, and/or not in their proper conditions.*

CHANGE: The balloon was full of air. Then it was empty.

TIME: I lit the candle. Several hours later it went out.

Once these basic concepts are mastered, your student will be on the road to solving learning or behavioral problems that stem from not knowing them.

A B C D E F G H I

J K L M N O P Q R

S T U V W X Y Z

Here are the upper and lowercase letters used for basic Symbol Mastery at the Davis Dyslexia Correction Center. They were specially designed for modeling in clay. Enlarge these pages at about 150 percent on a photocopier, then cut each copy into three strips. Tape them together to make long strips that look like these:

A B C D E F G H I J K L M N O P Q R S T U V W X Y Z

zyxwvutsrqponmlkjihgfedcba

zyxwvuts
rqponmlkji
hgfedcba

CHAPTER 16

Establishing Order

In our daily lives, most of us don't experience the chaos of nature. So we don't understand the importance of establishing order. As we go through our days, we don't notice how much and how often we are engaged in the activity of establishing order. We just do what we do, and life goes on. However, if we are truly going to be responsible—to engage in making significant, lasting change—we must be able to determine what the order should be. And we must be able to establish it.

It is important for any person with a learning problem to have the ability to establish order. This is especially true for individuals with ADD and math problems, because for these problems to exist, the individual must have an incorrect concept of order, or it could be missing altogether. The ability to establish order begins with an accurate concept of what order is and the skill to create what it is supposed to be. Actually, the act of correcting a problem is the act of establishing order.

Defining order is important to our understanding of

what it is. But understanding what the word *order* means won't in itself enable someone to *establish* order.

By our definition, order exists when things are in their proper places, proper positions, and proper conditions. What constitutes a proper place, a proper position, or a proper condition? Well, a place is simply a location in space relevant to its surroundings. A position is an attitude that an object occupies within a given space. And a condition? Well, that one is a little more complex. According to science, all things are continuously changing. There is a beginning and an end for all things. So during the era between a thing's beginning and its end, it exists in a continuum of change. A thing's condition is established by where it is within its continuum of change. Its condition is its state of existence. All of that seems simple enough.

It is the word "proper" that complicates order. For our purposes we'll use the popular British usage of the word where it means *fitting* or *suitable*. So we have the idea of a *fitting* or *suitable* place, position, and condition for something.

Therefore, before order can be established, someone must decide what the proper order should be. What all this boils down to is *who* decides what the fitting or suitable place, position, and condition is or should be?

It cannot be nature. In nature, all things exist in their places, positions, and conditions relative to the forces that put them there. In nature, disorder does not really exist. Clearly, the ideas of order and disorder are man-made concepts. If so, it is mankind that must decide what order is or should be. More specifically, in your own environment, it is *you* who must decide. You are the one who chooses what the fitting or suitable places, positions, and conditions for your things are or should be.

Establishing Order

We can liken "establishing order" to putting together a jigsaw puzzle, because that is exactly what you are doing. You dump the pieces on the table and what exists is chaos. The pieces are in a random state of disorder. The first thing most people do is spread out the pieces so none are on top of others. The next step is to turn over the pieces that landed upside down. Next is to find and isolate recognizable pieces. Because the border pieces have a straight edge, they are easily recognizable, so most people cull them out and group them together by color patterns. Then, based on their perimeter configuration, they are pieced together. Then the field is filled in by searching for pieces of the correct color patterns and perimeter configurations, and fitting them into the puzzle one at a time. When the last piece is placed in its proper place and position, the puzzle is complete.

Keep in mind that how the finished puzzle was supposed to look was predetermined. The order had been decided before the box was even opened. It was the act of putting the pieces where they should go that established the order. That was the act of establishing order.

We are not born with an inherent ability to establish order. It is something we must learn. We are supposed to learn it from the examples set by our parents and teachers. We are supposed to learn how to do it without understanding what it is. We are supposed to do it simply because we are expected to. If we want to see how well that has worked, we need look no further than the state of our jails and penitentiaries, or our ghettos. Most of us parents don't have to look any further than our child's bedroom.

Regarding the typical chaos of a child's room, the dynamics of the situation go beyond the mess. On the surface, it would appear that the child is simply a slob. The child has been told that it is his responsibility to keep his room in order, but doesn't do it. The parent is frustrated, and the child feels picked on. Usually, both the mess in the child's room and the frustration of the parent are products of three mistakes made by the parent:

1. *The child was told it is his responsibility to keep his room in order, yet the parent still attempts to control the situation.* The responsibility wasn't truly given to the child. If it had been, the parent wouldn't be frustrated by the condition of the room.

2. *The child wasn't capable or willing to assume responsibility.* If the child were truly capable and willing to be responsible for the order of his room, the parent would have nothing to complain about.

3. *It is the order determined by the parent, not by the child, that he is expected to maintain.* The child isn't

putting the things in the "proper" places where the parents want them, so the room is a mess—in their view. The child didn't determine what the order should be in the first place. If he had, and were truly responsible for it, the problem wouldn't exist.

If he's willing to learn, we should be able to teach a child how to establish order in his room. If he could do it there, he could do it anywhere. By knowing how to establish order, the individual can be truly responsible for creating a new order for things and situations that affect his life.

Creating Order

Order is created by first determining what the order should be, then establishing it. The three exercises that follow teach how to create order by assembling a fifty-piece jigsaw puzzle, how to determine order by cleaning a messy desk, and how to create order in the person's own space.

EXERCISE ONE
This exercise will introduce the fundamental steps of establishing order. You'll need an age-appropriate jigsaw puzzle. The puzzle should not contain more pieces than can easily be assembled in two hours, but should be large enough to require at least half an hour. A fifty-piece puzzle should be sufficient. You should perform the exercise in well-lit space, on a table or desk.

Put the puzzle on the table or desk, and have the student stand across the table from you. If appropriate, have the student check orientation (Chapter 9), do Release (Chapter 10), and set his Energy Dial (Chapter 13).

Use age-appropriate language but do not join in the activity—sit on your hands if you must.

1. Tell the student, *"We are going to establish order with a jigsaw puzzle. You may already know how to put a puzzle together, but I want you to follow my directions for doing it."*

2. Instruct the student to dump the contents of the box out on the table.

3. When done, instruct the student to separate the pieces so that none are on top of others.

4. When done, instruct the student to turn all the pieces faceup.

5. When done, instruct the student to search for and isolate the edge pieces into groups of similar color patterns.

6. When done or nearly done, instruct the student on how to assemble the adjoining edge pieces, based on color patterns and edge configuration.

7. Instruct the student to assemble the edge pieces together.

8. When done, point to a spot just inside one of the corners, and ask, *"What colors would the piece have to be that goes right here?"* When answered, ask, *"And what shape would it have to have?"*

9. When answered, say, *"Find that piece and put it in its place."*

10. Repeat steps 8 and 9 three times.

11. When done, ask, *"Can you pick the place where you want to put the next piece?"* If or when the answer is yes, instruct the student to do so. If no, repeat steps 8 through 11 until the answer is yes.

12. Have the student continue until the last piece is in place. When done say, *"Congratulations, you have established the order of this jigsaw puzzle! Now let's review exactly what you did. What was the first thing you did?"*

13. Review each step of the process through step 10 then ask, *"What was the last thing that you did?"*

14. When answered, say, *"That is a sequence for establishing order. With that sequence, or sometimes with some slight variation of it, you can establish order in anything as long as you know what order you are supposed to establish. If you don't know what order you are supposed to establish, then you have to determine that part on your own. Next we will do an exercise to show you how to do that."*

EXERCISE TWO

In this exercise, we will be introducing the fundamental steps of determining order. Once again, you'll need a well-lit table or desk. You'll also need about a dozen miscellaneous items from around the room, including some wadded-up tissues and scraps of paper. Set up your workspace. Put the miscellaneous items in a pile on the table or desk.

1. Instruct the student to pick an item from the pile.

2. Ask, *"What is it?"*

3. When answered, ask, *"What is its condition?"* Some of the condition variables could be:

- old or new
- good or bad
- dirty or clean
- broken or whole
- pretty or ugly
- or simply just okay

4. Ask, *"Where would a good place be, for that* [object] *in that condition?"*

5. When answered, say, *"Assign that object to that place by telling it that is its place."*

6. When done, ask, *"What position should that* [object], *in that condition, be in when it's in that place?"*

7. When done, say, *"Assign that* [object] *to that position in that place by telling it that is its position."*

8. When done, say, *"Put the* [object] *in its proper place, in its proper position."*

9. Repeat steps 1 through 8 for each item in the pile.

10. When the last item is placed, say, *"Congratulations, you have determined the order for and established the order of all those objects! With the sequence you followed you could determine and establish order in any environment."* There are nine steps in the sequence. They are:

(1) Isolate an individual thing;
(2) identify what it is;
(3) determine its condition;
(4) based on its identity and condition, determine the best place for it to be in;
(5) assign it that place;
(6) determine what position it should occupy in that place;
(7) assign it that position;
(8) put it in that position in that place.
(9) Repeat this sequence until order is established in the environment.

11. Have the student write down the above sequence. When done, say *"That is your instruction guide for creating order. With that sequence you* *could go into any environment that needs order and create it. There is one more exercise we will do that will allow you to practice creating order."*

EXERCISE THREE

Now we are going to teach the student how to create order. You will need to perform this exercise in a room in the student's home, preferably his own bedroom. If you are working with an older student or an adult, let the student choose the room. Use all of the existing contents of the room. The student should have the instruction guide he wrote for creating order.

If your student is a child who isn't your own, you must explain what you are going to do to his parent and get permission. Explain to the student that he is going to be creating order in his space. It will be a new order—it will be his order. Now, go to the room.

Before you begin, if the room is cluttered with all kinds of "stuff" strewn on the floor, have the student pile it all in the middle of the room or just outside the room.

1. Begin with the largest piece of furniture in the room. Touch the object and ask, *"What is this?"*

2. When answered, ask, *"What is its condition?"*

3. When answered, ask, *"Is this a good place for it, or should it be somewhere else?"*

• If the object is okay where it is say, *"Assign*

it that place and position by telling it this is your place and your position."

- If it must be moved ask, *"Where would you want it to be?"* When answered, say, *"Assign it that place by telling it that is its place."*
- When done, ask, *"What position should it have in that place?"* When answered, say, *"Assign it that position by telling it that is its position."*
- If it must be moved say, *"Let's move it, I'll help you."* Help the student to put the object where he wants it. Of course, you should use your common sense. If it's a grand piano, you may need some help. Or if it is a bookshelf, the student may need to remove the books in order to lighten the load. If there are items in the place where he wants it to be, ask him to clear the space first.

4. Repeat steps 1 through 3 on the rest of the large objects in the room. Large objects are pieces of furniture, or objects that sit on the furniture, like a TV on a chest of drawers or a computer on a desk.

5. When you're finished with all the large objects, have the student start on the little stuff. Say, *"You have your instruction guide to follow for creating order. What is the first instruction?"* When the student answers, *"Isolate an individual thing."* Say, *"Do that—isolate an individual thing."* Have the student pick up something. There will probably be a pile of stuff in the middle of the room or just outside the door from which to choose.

6. Say, *"Follow the steps on your instruction guide for that thing."* You may need to assist the student with some hints like, *"Most people assign dirty socks to a laundry hamper,"* or *"Most people assign clean underwear to a place and position in a drawer."*

7. When the student has done step 8 and "Put it there," ask, *"You have assigned that* [condition, object] *to a place and position, is that the place and position for all* [condition, objects]*?"*

8. If or when the answer is yes, say, *"Just like doing the jigsaw puzzle, find all the* [condition, objects] *and put them in their place and position."*

9. When done, ask, *"What does step nine on your instruction guide say?"* When answered with *"Repeat this sequence until order is established in the environment,"* say, *"Okay, start with number one again."*

10. Repeat steps 6 through 8 until there is order. Observe the student. If he is working on the tenth object or so, and still referring to the guide, you can ask, *"Can you remember the steps so you don't have to keep referring to your guide?"* The goal here is for the steps to become a part of the student's identity. You may need to assist him in committing the sequence to memory by challenging him to remember what the next step is before he reads it.

11. You may not need to remain there for the entire process of creating order. If the student is doing it without any assistance from you ask, *"Do you still need me, or can you finish this job on your own?"* If the student feels that you're still needed, remain there.

12. If you are no longer needed, or when the job is completed, end the exercise by saying, *"Everything in this space, or that comes into this space, must be assigned its order. It is your responsibility to do that. It's your space, so it's your duty to do it. Also, it's your duty and responsibility to maintain the order. That means when something is out of its place or its position or its condition, you are the one who reestablishes the order by putting it where it belongs. It's your job, and if you do your job well, no one can complain."*

SECTION THREE

Addressing
ADD and ADHD

CHAPTER 17

A Correction Strategy for ADD and ADHD

There is a simple truth: *If you eliminate the reason a problem exists, the problem will cease to exist.* This is the foundation of our ADD correction strategy. By definition, ADD exists because of two components— the developmental aspect and the disorientation aspect. So our strategy addresses both fronts.

We can now create a plan of action. It will consist of *why* something must be done, *what* to do, and *when* to do it. The *how to do it* steps, the actual procedures, are referenced by chapter numbers. For now, let's assemble a "map"—our blueprint for eliminating the recognized ADD behaviors.

The behaviors that need to be addressed are associated with impulsivity, inattention, and hyperactivity:

- *difficulty taking turns*
- *acting before thinking*
- *difficulty staying seated and sitting still*

- *running or climbing on things excessively*
- *problems organizing work*
- *constant shifting from one activity to another*
- *failure to finish tasks started*
- *easy distractibility*
- *seeming lack of attention*
- *difficulty concentrating on tasks requiring sustained attention*

The goal is to help a student establish new behaviors that will supplant these unwanted behaviors. All behavior is manifested to support a person's identity. The identity is a product of the filtering system described in Chapter 2. It is composed of *real knowledge* that came from life experiences. The content of the filtering system influences the individual's perception of, and reaction to, the environment. It dictates the behavior of the individual. So the student's filtering system must be the target of our efforts.

Give and Take

We want to change the content of an existing system. Theoretically, there are only two ways this could be done: We could either add something or take something away. The filtering system is composed of real knowledge that is already in place. We have no way of removing any of it, so if we want to change it at all, the only possible way would be to add something to it. In essence, we will need to add new knowledge that will override or supplant the old knowledge, and thereby change the behavior. Luckily for us, the learning process is capable of making this happen.

The challenge is getting the new knowledge past the existing filtering system, which by its nature will attempt to filter out anything that conflicts with what is already there.

We need to go about this in two stages:

1. Install new knowledge that, in itself, does not conflict with the existing content of the system. This means adding small, separate pieces of new knowledge independent of each other. The Concept Mastery procedure in Chapter 15 is a way to accomplish this.

2. Link the independent pieces together once they are in place within the system. This can be accomplished by establishing a new order, as explained later in this chapter.

The system used by Davis Dyslexia Correction Facilitators works very well. Below is the step-by-step sequence of the procedures.

The first step, as with any other job, is preparation. We need to prepare ourselves for the tasks we are about to perform. Right now as you are reading this, you are preparing to do something. You are in the process of assembling the information, instructions, and tools you will need. Once your own preparation process is complete, you will need to prepare your student for the activities he or she will need to perform.

Install the Basic Tools

Your student must be willing to cooperate in this endeavor. If the student isn't motivated, you won't even be able to start. Use the information on Motivation in Chapter 7 of the Basic Tools section to aid you in motivating your student.

You'll need to give the student a tool that allows him to be mentally present with you as you guide him through the processes. In order to facilitate the student's progress, he must experience the same real-world environment as you. The student must be in an oriented state while the new knowledge is installed, so you must provide a tool to control disorientation. Use the Perceptual Ability Assessment procedure in Chapter 8 to help you decide which of the orientation techniques to use, then perform the appropriate procedure, either Davis Orientation Counseling in Chapter 9 or Alignment in Chapter 12.

Once the student can share the same reality as you, he will need a couple of tools that will make it comfortable for him to remain there. The Release procedure in Chapter 10 will allow him to eliminate feelings of stress and tension. The Dial Setting procedure in Chapter 13 will enable him to adjust his energy level and the speed of his internal clock.

Stage One

Once these tools are in place, the two of you can begin addressing the problems. In this first of two stages, you will install information into the student's filtering system that is different from his previous life experience. To accomplish this, you will use the processes and follow the sequence described in the Concept Mastery procedure in Chapter 15.

Here are the concepts and the sequence of addressing them:

Self: *a model representing himself, which represents all of the knowledge, wisdom, and understanding gained throughout his lifetime.*

Change: *something becoming something else.*

Consequence: *something that happens as a result of something else.*

Cause: *something that makes something else happen.*

Effect: *something that happened as a result of something else.*

Before: *happening earlier.*

After: *happening later.*

Time: *the measurement of change in relation to a standard.*

Sequence: *the way things follow each other one after another in size, amount, time, arbitrary order, or importance.*

Order: *things in their proper places, proper positions, and proper conditions.* (There is also a definition of "order" that means "sequence," but for our purposes we will keep the two concepts separate.)

Disorder: *things not in their proper places, their proper positions, or their proper conditions.*

First, follow the instructions in Chapter 15 and have the student master these concepts. Once they are inserted into the student's filtering system, the first stage will be complete and Stage Two can begin. This is where you will help the student link the individual concepts together. In turn, this will allow the student to eliminate or correct the ADD behaviors.

Stage Two

Now you are going to link the individual concepts of Stage One together. The goal is to have the student establish a new order of behaviors.

PERSONALIZE THE CONCEPTS

You can do this by having the student actually use the new concepts. At this point the student has completed concept mastery of *order*. The next step would be to have the student experience establishing order. Follow the instructions laid out in Chapter 16. In performing the exercises, the student adds experiential knowledge and begins to develop his skill in creating order. This begins the process of linking the concepts and establishes a foundation for addressing individual behaviors.

The next step is to address the behaviors. The student is now ready to apply his new knowledge and skill to establishing a new order for his behavior. The same basic principles for determining and establishing order apply to both objects and activities. Of course the technique is different, but the reasoning, logic, and strategy are the same. The problem is that the existing order of behaviors is dictated by the person's identity. While going through these exercises, the new concepts will link together in the filtering system causing a change in identity. This then will allow the student to change the activity (behavior).

This can be done by having the student go through the clay modeling and discussion part of the Concept Mastery procedure again, creating the concept of *consequence*. However, this time you will have the student model one of his own ADD behaviors. The clay models will be scenarios showing sequences of events. He will create sequences of cause and effect scenarios showing how activity [A] caused a resulting activity

230 The Gift of Learning

[B], which in turn caused activity [C], and so on. The models must show how whatever he did in the first scenario led to the undesirable effect in the final one. He must then describe or explain it to you.

DEALING WITH THE BASIC CAUSES

Impulsivity, inattention, and hyperactivity are the root causes, in whole or in part, of all the behaviors associated with ADD (see the list of behaviors at the beginning of this chapter). One or more of these three fundamental behavior patterns underlies all the rest of the behaviors that need to be addressed.

The behavioral activity is something the student actually *does* that is considered a problem. For example, the act of pushing another child out of the way to get to the front of a line, yelling out an answer, or getting out of a chair and running around the room. So it is the actual activity of the student that needs to be addressed. In working with a real-life situation, compiling a list of these behavioral activities should be quite easy—it's whatever gets the student into trouble or makes other people react negatively.

These unproductive or antisocial activities should be addressed one at a time. At first, choose only those that can be easily linked to the motivation of the student. If the motivation is "wanting someone to like me," choose a behavior that obviously causes others not to like him.

In creating the scenarios, your student will get to the point where he realizes that his activity produces a consequence—an effect he doesn't like. He must see the cause-and-effect relationship linking something he *does* to something he *does not* like or want for himself.

What is perfectly obvious to a parent won't be apparent to a child who lacks the concept of consequence.

Say an ADD child grabs a toy away from another child, and the other child begins to cry. Then the teacher comes and scolds the ADD child and makes him give it back. After that, the other child won't even talk to him. He needs to link the effect of the other child ignoring him to the cause of his having grabbed the toy away.

Once the student links his behavior as a cause to the negative effect he experienced, he will be ready, willing, and able to alter his behavior. What actually occurs is that the student alters his filtering system in the direction of having accurate basic concepts of the ideas listed earlier. Eventually, these new concepts will link together to replace and override whatever was previously there. The student has discovered the cause of the negative effect. He is willing to establish a new order of behavior.

Then, have the student model a similar activity with a different behavior on his part, one that produces a desirable effect. He will create a model of a new order of behavior. Now he can clearly see how to cause a desired effect by performing an alternate activity (behaving differently). He is able to incorporate this new knowledge into his filtering system.

BEHAVIOR CHOICES

Now he has two potential behavioral activities in his filtering system. Next, he needs real-life reinforcement of the new behavior. Once experience proves that the new knowledge works better, it will override the old knowledge. The student will have established a new order of behavior, and the old knowledge will no longer be a dominant part of his identity.

Follow these steps with the same process, using another ADD behavior. When that one is complete, do another one. Continue this for as long as necessary. Sooner or later, depending on the student, he will reach the point of making a major shift. He will begin to perceive himself as the primary cause of what he likes and doesn't like. At this point, his filtering system has changed. He has an accurate concept of *consequence* overriding whatever other concept was there before.

You will recognize the shift when it occurs. While modeling an activity that produces a negative effect, the student will tell you what the alternate activity would have to be. At this point, you will not need to address any more negative behaviors. Trust the student to make whatever further adjustments are needed on his own.

Once this shift occurs, you and your student have successfully addressed one of the two fronts of the ADD problem.

DISORIENTATION

Next, it's time to address the spontaneous disorientation aspect of ADD. As I said in Chapter 3, the student's hyperactivity or hypoactivity, impulsivity, and inattention are either influenced by, or are products of disorientation.

By using Alignment or the Orientation procedure you will have already given the student the tools he needs to correct disorientation. If you followed the instructions correctly, your student should have fine-tuned this tool to the point of having optimum perception while oriented. Using Release, he will also have the ability to release tension and stress. And he should also be able to control his energy level and perception of time using the Dial Setting procedure.

The student needs to know how and when to use these tools in order to prevent or eliminate a negative effect. There are two important points to get across: consciously using Orientation or Alignment to get a clear view of things, and adjusting the Energy Dial level to achieve rapport with another person or a group of people. The student must have the responsibility for using the tools. You must help him gain the knowledge and skill to do so.

Your job here is to advise, remind, and encourage

the student to use the tools. As you are working, you can do this by asking him to check his orientation or alignment if you see it's needed. If the energy is too high or too low, ask if the dial is set right for the current activity. If stress or tension begins to creep in, ask if it's a good time to do Release. By asking instead of telling you are not taking responsibility away from the student—you are giving it to him.

In essence, we see the spontaneous disorientation aspect of ADD as a negative effect coming from a positive ability. We want the student to eliminate the negative effect without inhibiting the positive ability. The simplest way is to treat the negative effect like any other behavior.

ENERGY CONSERVATION
For hyperactivity and hypoactivity, have the student go through the clay and discussion part of the Concept Mastery procedure for *consequence*—showing an activity performed in an oriented state, and then in a disoriented state. Do the same thing showing an activity performed at different dial settings. Have the student make a list of daily activities, then ask him to determine the best dial setting for each activity. He may need to change the settings on the list after trying them out in real life. That's understandable, and it demonstrates that he is actually using the tools.

The impulsivity aspect of ADD, stemming mostly from the developmental track, has already been covered, except for *constant shifting from one activity to another.* In Chapter 3, this was attributed to disorientation. It is part of the inattention component of ADD.

In addressing inattention, we must realize that there will be some characteristics we won't be able to change. We may have some influence over the frequency of occurrence and the intensity of certain activities, but eliminating them is undesirable if not impossible. We won't be able to reduce or eliminate the intelligence, environmental awareness, curiosity, or creativity of the student without using drugs. In fact, by giving him the tools to address his behavior, we may have enhanced these qualities. Overall, we should consider that a good thing.

Finishing Touches

By addressing *failure to finish tasks started* and *shifting from one activity to another,* we have already made inroads. After mastering the behavioral concepts, the student will be able to conceive of causing a change. He will be able to understand the idea of *finishing* something. The student is also prepared with the concepts of *time, sequence,* and *order.* Even though he may need a little more practice in establishing order in the environment, he can now understand that completing a task is actually the final step in establishing order.

This student will be capable of finishing tasks, even if distractibility is still a factor. He will inherently understand that the purpose of doing something is to finish it.

Even with all this in place, if the student isn't motivated to do a particular task, it probably won't get finished. Homework assigned by a teacher who doesn't first motivate the student to do it is an invitation for noncompliance. Motivating a child to do homework just so the teacher will like him may work temporarily, but not for long. You will probably need to find some other desire to motivate your student. At this stage at least, if the student fails to make good grades, he will understand why he didn't.

The *easy distractibility* part of ADD is where spontaneous disorientation comes into play. Mastering behaviors won't have much effect. The orientation tool or the alignment tool—whichever the student uses— will enable him to terminate a disorientation, but it will not prevent disorientation from occurring. Having the student go through the Concept Mastery procedure steps on the consequences of orientation and disorientation for certain activities should have some positive effect.

The Gift of Multitasking

We must keep in mind that natural curiosity is the stimulus for disorientations that cause distractibility. The student will not be able to eliminate that, and shouldn't want to. In time, and with a little practice, a student can learn to shift his attention consciously, without disorienting.

An original sculpture by Mark Steele,
courtesy of Intellution Software.

Not every shift of attention is caused by disorientation. But in a typical classroom, even a normal change of interest due to curiosity may be seen as such. The best solution for this is learning to multitask. This ability develops naturally, usually around the age of twelve. Telling a younger student that it is possible would be a first step in the right direction. I haven't developed specific exercises to facilitate this skill, but you may be able to accelerate its development.

There are any number of games you can play with a student to encourage multitasking. Something as simple as challenging your student to rub his tummy and pat his head at the same time is a move in the direction of multitasking. Challenging the student to repeat statements verbatim back to you while playing a video game or watching TV also pushes the limits. Challenging a child to do more than one thing at a time as often as you can, in as many ways as you can, will facilitate the development of multitasking.

If you choose to facilitate your student in developing the ability to multitask, please keep in mind that you may be letting a genie out of a bottle. I like that idea, because I don't think this particular genie should be kept bottled up.

Multitasking will relieve your student's distract-ibility somewhat, but the real solution would be to make what's happening in the classroom the most interesting thing in the environment for the student.

"Difficulty staying on task" (using our revised definition of "inattention") has now been fully addressed. You have your roadmap for addressing the common behaviors by which ADD is recognized. Your next step is the first step in actually doing it. Good luck!

SECTION FOUR

Addressing Math

Acalculia and Dyscalculia

CHAPTER 18

A Correction Strategy for Math

This chapter maps out a strategy for correcting *acalculia* and *dyscalculia*. It will detail *what* must be done, *when* to do it, and the reason *why*. The actual correction procedures are given in the next chapter.

As I said, there are two basic factors or components involved in both of these learning problems:

1. The developmental aspect, where the student has missing or incorrect concepts.

2. Inappropriate standard teaching methods, which don't work for students who think in pictures.

At the root of the developmental aspect of the problem is disorientation. It is a factor both directly and indirectly. Disorientation is the primary reason the student has missing or incorrect concepts. It can also interfere with any attempt to correct the situation. So to get to the root of the problem and correct it, disorientation must be addressed first.

There are three fronts to be addressed—disorientation, missing or inaccurate basic concepts, and inappropriate teaching methods—so we will address the problem in three stages. First, we will give the student the ability to establish and maintain his orientation. Next, we will help him install accurate basic concepts. Finally, we will teach him arithmetic in an appropriate way.

Stage One: Install the Basic Tools

As with any job, preparation comes first. As you read this, you are already preparing yourself for this task. By assembling the information, instruction, and tools you will need, you will become capable of doing the job. Once that process is complete, you will need to prepare your student for the activities that need to be performed. For this, you should follow the steps laid out for motivating your student in Chapter 7. When your student is adequately motivated, you can begin the process of correcting his problems with math.

The first step is to give your student a tool for being mentally present with you during the instruction. In order to learn new things, the student must be able to experience the same real-world environment as you, so the student must be in an *oriented* state while doing the exercises. There are two orientation tools to choose from: the Davis Orientation Counseling in Chapter 9 or Alignment in Chapter 12. The Perceptual Ability

Assessment, in Chapter 8, will help you decide which to use.

Once your student can experience the same reality as you, you will introduce a couple of tools that make it comfortable for him to remain there. The Release procedure in Chapter 10 will allow your student to let go of any feelings of stress and tension that come up. And the Dial Setting procedure in Chapter 13 will allow the student to adjust his own energy level and set the speed of his internal clock. Even if your student isn't a known disorienter, go ahead and provide him with the appropriate tools anyway.

Stage Two: Installing Accurate Basic Concepts

Now you and your student can begin addressing the next aspect—missing or inaccurate basic concepts. The student needs to have accurate basic concepts inherently installed in his identity. These will become a part of who the student is. It is fairly easy to *add* a missing concept, but *replacing* an inaccurate concept is a bigger challenge. The inaccurate concept is already an inherent part of the student's identity, so to him it seems absolutely true. In essence, the identity of the student must be changed to include the new, accurate concepts. To do this, you will use the process and follow the sequence laid out in the Concept Mastery procedure in Chapter 15.

Here are the concepts needed, and the sequence that works best, in addressing them:

self: *a model representing self, including all the knowledge, wisdom, and understanding of the person's lifetime.*

change: *something becoming something else.*

consequence: *something that happens as a result of something else.*

cause: *something that makes something else happen.*

effect: *something that happened as a result of something else.*

before: *happening earlier.*

after: *happening later.*

time: *the measurement of change in relation to a standard.*

sequence: *the way things follow each other one after another in size, amount, time, arbitrary order, and importance.*

order: *things in their proper places, proper positions, and proper conditions.*

disorder: *things not in their proper places, and/or not in their proper positions, and/or not in their proper conditions.*

When you follow the instructions in Chapter 15, you will have your student model all these concepts in clay. The next step is to follow the instructions in Chapter 16, "Establishing Order." After those exercises are completed, he will have integrated the basic concepts into his identity. Once the concepts are inherent to the identity of the student, the second stage is complete.

Stage Three: Install Arithmetic Concepts

Stage three involves teaching the student the principles of arithmetic. Here, the student must link the basic concepts to the objective of learning arithmetic. You can accomplish this by having him actually use the new concepts. He has already mastered the concept of order and has experienced the activity of establishing order. Now you should have him establish order for and with the objectives of math. Linking these basic concepts to arithmetic principles is only half the task. After that, your student will still need to make the conversion from picture-thinking arithmetic to doing it the conventional way, with a pencil.

The next chapter is a teaching guide for stage three, with step-by-step instructions.

CHAPTER 19

Twelve Exercises
for Teaching Math

There must be hundreds of different techniques for teaching math. Many are probably excellent, but because numbers and I have always been good friends, I haven't been exposed to any of them. I can't remember a time when a quadratic equation did not evoke a feeling of comfort within me. Maybe it is the shape of a square, or the idea of a limit to higher powers of unknown quantities, or maybe it's just because I think with pictures and find it easy to mentally manipulate shapes and quantities.

In the past, whenever I needed to teach math, I have always taught its simplicity and beauty. Because I am strictly a picture-thinker, I used a pictorial thinking style of instruction, and it has always worked. I am an engineer, so I also consider my strategy for teaching math to be well engineered.

I have broken the procedure down into twelve progressive steps that tell you exactly what I would do. Each is a series of exercises. At the beginning of each step is a brief statement of its objective and the reasoning behind it.

These twelve exercises are used by the network of professional Davis Facilitators around the world to effectively teach the principles of math to students with acalculia or dyscalculia. Don't be intimidated if you're not a wizard at math yourself; you don't need to be.

The exercises are presented here so you can become familiar with them. Once you have done the preparatory steps with your student as outlined in the last chapter, come back to this chapter and simply follow the recipe. As the student completes each sub-step, check it off and go on to the next one.

Motivation

Before you begin working with your student, remember the importance of motivation. If your student doesn't have a reason to learn math, even the best technique for teaching it won't work. I'll tell you what I and other professional Davis Facilitators normally do, but you are familiar with your own student, so adjust your language to fit your situation.

To motivate any student, we need to appeal to some emotion that will channel attention in the direction we want it to go, and create an intention to learn what we can teach. When I do it, I ask these three questions:

- "I understand you have a problem with math, is that right?" (The answer must be yes, before proceeding.)

- "Would you like to learn how to do math so it will be easy?" (Again, the answer must be yes.)

- "I think I could help you learn how to do math. Would you like to try?" (Once again, the answer must be yes.)

To help with motivation, see Chapter 7 for more suggestions. Once you have a motivated student, set up your work space. It's the same setup used for the Concept Mastery procedures in Chapter 15, which you should have done as part of your student's preparation. The materials you will need are:

- about two pounds of plasteline clay,

- a plastic knife, and

- several sheets of paper and a pencil. However, keep the pencil and paper hidden away. The student won't use them and doesn't need to see them until the final exercise.

Math Exercise 1
Make Sure the Student Can Count

Counting is the act of determining a quantity. A change has occurred, and the act of counting is measuring that change using a numeration system as a standard. The act of counting is an expression of the concepts of *time, sequence,* and *order* versus *disorder.*

The principal concept of time is the measurement of change in relation to a standard. Counting must be performed in a numeration sequence, meaning the way things follow each other one after another. And some order must be established wherein the balls, that have been counted are excluded from those that have not yet been counted. Both counted and uncounted balls must be placed in their proper places, positions, and conditions. So the act of counting is an expression of the concepts of *time, sequence,* and *order* versus *disorder.*

PROCEDURE

- Begin by making about 30 small balls rolled from clay (you will eventually need one hundred). You and your student can make them together. Put about 12 balls on the table in front of the student and ask, "How many?"

- Watch carefully to see how the student separates and counts the balls. If the student has any difficulty with this you should model the activity for him. Separate the balls so none are touching each other, and touch each ball as you count them out. When the student can accurately follow your model, go to the next step.

- In the worst-case scenario you may need to teach the student the numeration system. Do this by

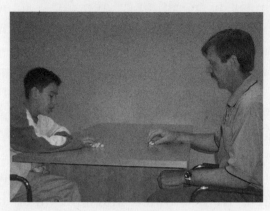

Counting. You can model this activity if need be.

using Davis Symbol Mastery: Have the student put 1 ball on the table. Under it, put the numeral 1 and the word *one*. Do the verbal steps of Symbol Mastery on both the numeral and the word. Then do the concept of 2. You may need to go all the way to 100, or the student may get the idea much earlier. Once the student can recite the numeration system sequence with certainty you can continue.

Note: If you have to start with teaching the numeration system, the whole process may take a week or longer. Once the student appears to have no problem counting the balls you toss on the table, go to the next exercise.

Math Exercise 2
Challenge the Student's Ability to Establish Order

The student must have confidence in his ability to establish order despite your interference. His ability to establish order must be greater than your ability to establish disorder. This gives the student a higher degree of control, reinforces his ability to establish order, and reinforces his motivation.

PROCEDURE

- Playfully toss a few more balls into the ones he has just counted and ask, "How many?"

- As the student starts to recount, playfully toss a few more balls into the counted ones and ask again, "How many?" Keep it playful and don't let the student get too frustrated. If the student simply starts recounting this time, you may wish to reach over and remove a few balls from the ones he has counted and ask again, "How many?" If the student gives you an answer, challenge the answer by saying, "Are you sure?" and "Count them again."

- Keep doing this activity, adding and removing balls, until the student realizes he must do something that will prevent you from interfering. It is best if the student realizes on his own that he must put the counted balls into a place where you cannot interfere. If it seems that he is not getting there and getting very frustrated, you may need to

Eventually, the student will figure out how to prevent you from changing the number of balls to be counted.

lead him to the realization. You could ask, "Where could you put them so I couldn't interfere?"

Note: After the student is putting the balls in a place where you cannot interfere, continue to try to interfere. Continuing to try unsuccessfully will increase the student's emotional satisfaction at winning this game, and firmly establish his control. Acknowledge that the student won, and take a short break before you continue.

Math Exercise 3
Introduce the Concepts of Adding and Subtracting

In this exercise, we want to assess whether or not the student can add and subtract with certainty. We don't need to teach what the student already knows. If the student already knows how to do this, we must get through it quickly so the student doesn't get bored. We also want to increase the degree of the student's control.

PROCEDURE

- From the big pile of balls put three balls in front of you and instruct the student by saying, "Do what I do."

- When the student puts out three balls, ask, "How many?" If there is any delay in answering say, "Count them." If the student includes yours in their count, say, "Only count your own." If the student "protects" the counted ones, say, "You already won the order game, so I'm not going to play it anymore."

- Proceed only after the student gives the correct answer. Put one more ball with the others in front of you.

- When the student does the same, ask, "How many?" If there is any hesitation, say, "Count them."

- Add two or three more. When the student follows again, ask, "How many?" Continue this activity until the student can answer with certainty.

- Next, go through the process in reverse by removing balls and asking, "How many?" Continue this activity until the student can answer with certainty.

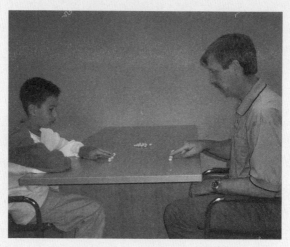

When the student can answer the question "How many?"
without hesitation, continue.

- End the activity by saying, "Well, you certainly can add and subtract." Take a break before you continue.

Math Exercise 4
Introduce the Concept of Counting in Multiples

In this exercise, we want to establish the foundation of multiplication as adding in groups. Take breaks as necessary.

PROCEDURE
- Between the two of you, put out three rows of two balls each, about one-half-inch apart, and ask, "Can you count by twos?"

"six!" ⬤ ⬤ "five"

"four!" ⬤ ⬤ "three"

"two!" ⬤ ⬤ "one"

Note that if you are sitting across the table from the student, the order of your demonstration will be moving from left to right and top to bottom.

- If the student says, "Yes," say, "Show me."

- If the student cannot show you, model it for him. Touch the nearest right ball and quietly say, "one," then touch the left ball, and a little louder, say, "two." Then touch the middle-row right ball and quietly say, "three," then the left ball, and a little louder, say, "four." Follow the pattern for the top row, then say, "You do it."

- When the student can accurately do it, go on.

- Ask, "Can you count by threes?" If "Yes" say, "Show me." If not, model it as before beginning with nearest right ball and go up instead of sideways. When the student can accurately do it, go on.

- Add three balls to each row of two and make another row of five so there are four rows of five. Ask, "Can you count by fours?" Follow the model on page 256.

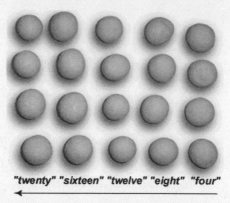

"twenty" "sixteen" "twelve" "eight" "four"

Diagrams of these math problems are from the helper's perspective, with the student sitting across the table.

- Ask, "Can you do it without saying all of them?" If the student can, go on.

- If not, model by touching the right-side column, and say "four," move left one column, say, "eight." Do each column one at a time. Then say, "You do it." Even if the student goes slowly and is silently doing it one at a time, accept it and go on.

- Ask, "Can you do fives?" Follow the above models.

Math Exercise 5
Introduce Counting Backward in Multiples

The purpose of this exercise is to establish the foundation of division as subtracting in groups. Remember to take breaks as necessary.

PROCEDURE

- Ask, "Can you count backward?" If "Yes," say, "Show me, count backward from ten." If not, model it by adding five more balls to the nearest row of five and then counting them backward from ten. Continue when the student can accurately do it.

- Ask, "Can you do it with fives?" If "Yes," say, "Show me." Point to the four rows of five and say, "From these twenty, count backward." If not, model it and have the student do it. When the student can accurately do it, go on.

- Ask, "Can you do it with fours?" Follow the above model (you may need to remove some of the balls to make five rows of four). When the student can accurately do it, go on.

Math Exercise 6
Introduce Multiplication Using a Grid

By utilizing the shape of a square, with the patterns that can be created within it, the student can use picture thinking when determining quantities. Multiplication actually has reason supporting it. It is not composed of rote memory as taught in school. I want the student to know why $9 \times 9 = 81$, with the ability to prove it with certainty, and not just remember it.

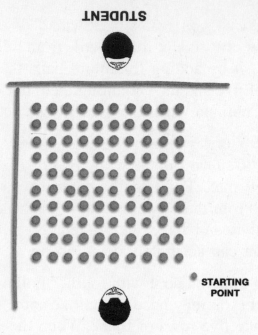

STUDENT

STARTING
POINT

TEACHER

The modeling you will do will be upside down and backward
for you, but will be right-side up and forward for the student.
If you cannot think and function from this perspective, you
should sit side-by-side with the student. The illustrations show
the helper's view sitting across the table with the student
working from his upper-left corner.

PROCEDURE

- Say, "Let's create a square shape with ten rows of
  ten in each row." You can use the ropes of clay
  to make sure the rows and columns are straight.
  You can help make the grid if the student is
  having any difficulty. You want the grid to be
  "reasonably" square.

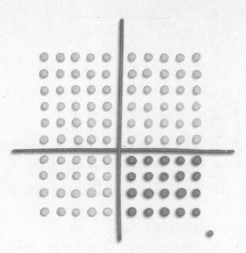

Four times five equals twenty.

- Ask, "If you were going to count them, where would you start?" Add a small dab of clay near that corner, and say, "That is just to tell me where your starting point is."

- From the start point, count up or down four rows and lay a rope across the grid, then from the same corner count over five columns and lay another rope. Point to the quadrant and ask, "How many?" If there is any hesitation say, "Count them."

- If the student answers immediately, or after he has counted, ask, "Are you sure?" If the student is unsure, say, "Count them again." Again ask, "Are you sure?"

- When he says he is sure, say, "Prove it." If/when the student asks, "How?" say, "Count them out loud to me." When finished, say, "You are right, I agree there are exactly twenty balls there."

- After a short break, wave your hand over the grid and say, "If you look at the whole grid you see that there are four sections to it.

- Ask, "Do you know how many balls there are in the whole grid?" If the student doesn't know, have him, or you model, counting the ten rows by tens.

- If he answers 100, ask, "How do you know?" When he answers, say, "Prove it, count it out loud by tens." When complete, say, "You are exactly correct, and I agree that there are exactly one hundred balls in the grid."

- Ask, "If there are one hundred in the whole grid, and there are twenty in this section (point to the quadrant), how many are out here?" Wave your hand over the rest of the whole grid.

- If the student doesn't know, say, "There are eighty, and I can prove it." If the student answers "eighty," say, "You are exactly right, and I can prove it." Model counting the perimeter of a quadrant and counting by multiples for the quadrant.

- For example, count from the rope and say, "There are six this way." Count over from the corner to the rope and say, "There are five this way." Count in units of six one way, and count in units of five

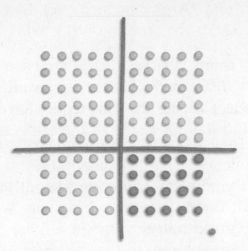

Five times four equals twenty.

the other way, each time arriving at thirty, and say, "There are thirty here."

- After counting out the three quadrants say, "Now all I have to do is add; there are thirty here, and thirty here. Thirty and thirty are sixty, so there are sixty here. There are twenty here. Twenty and sixty are eighty, so there are eighty left out here."

- Say, "I proved it, now you prove it." Have the student do it. Honor the accomplishment with dignity.

- Take a break.

- Remove the ropes from the grid, and say, "Count over four and lay the rope down." When done, say, "Count (up or down) from the start point five and lay the rope across." When done ask, "How many?" and "Are you sure?" and then say, "Prove it."

- Say, "Twenty, that's exactly what we had before; what is different?" If there is any difficulty with the student seeing the difference, have him move around to the other side of the table and the view of the grid will be the same as before.

- After the student can state the difference, ask, "Then it doesn't matter which way we go, if we have five and four the answer is twenty, correct?" Watch for certainty in the student's answer.

- Remove the ropes and say, "Count over three and put the rope down." When done, say, "Count (up or down) three, and put the rope across." When done, ask, "How many?" and "Are you sure?" and "Could you prove it if I asked you to?" If the answer is "Yes" with certainty in the voice, go on. If not, say, "Then prove it." When done, go on.

- Say, "Then three, [count (up or down) the three to the rope] *times* three, (count over three to the rope) is nine." Ask, "Correct?" The answer must be yes.

   Note: You have just given the student a functional definition for the word *times*.

- Wave your hand over the grid and say, "Then this grid is a *real* times table, and we can prove it." Say, "Move the ropes to show four times four." When done, ask, "What's four times four?" When

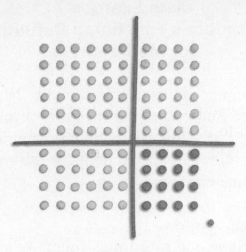

Four times four equals sixteen.

answered, ask, "Why?" If the student can't answer, answer for him. Say, "Four times four is sixteen because that's how many there are in here (point to the quadrant) and if you don't believe me you can count them yourself!"

- Say, "Show me five times five." Ask, "What's five times five?" and "Why is five times five twenty-five?"

- Go all the way through the times table, intermittently asking, "Are you sure?" and "Prove it."

Make sure you take a good break before moving on.

Math Exercise 7
Introduce a Functional Definition
for Mathematics

At this point, the student should have enough experience to understand the meaning of mathematics, so it's time to give him a functional definition of math. The goal is to prepare the student for learning division, using the same clay grid.

PROCEDURE

- Say, "Show me four times four." When the ropes are set, say, "When we have this kind of shape and construction, there are three pieces of information here. They are: How many are *here* (count up or down to the rope four), how many are *here* (count over to the rope four), and how many are *in here* (wave your hand over the quadrant, sixteen)."

- Say, "If we can count, and if we know what two of the three pieces of information are, we can always figure out what that third piece of information is." Ask, "Right?"

- Say, *"All mathematics is, is figuring out the third piece of information."*

- Say, "That statement is very simple but it is true. Any time we are doing math, no matter what kind of math it is, all we must do is figure out the third piece of information. If it is adding, we have a piece of information like we have two balls, and we have another piece of information like we put three more balls with them, then the third piece of information is five. We can either count to find the answer, or after a while we will just remember the answer. Subtracting is the same thing, only backward. We have one piece of information like we have ten balls, then we have another piece of information like somebody took three of them away, then the third piece of information would be how many are left, seven. Seven is the answer, because it is the third piece of information. We just did multiplication and all we were doing was figuring out the third piece of information. Every answer you gave me was only the third piece of information. Does that make sense to you?" Make sure the student really understands this concept.

- Point to the quadrant and ask, "If we have this piece of information (sweep your finger up the edge), and this piece of information (sweep your finger across the bottom), what is the third piece of information?" If the student says, "Sixteen." Say, "That is the right answer for this example, because in concept sixteen is how many are here. The third piece of information is how many are in here (wave your hand over the quadrant)."

- Ask, "What if we already had this piece of information (wave your hand over the quadrant), and this piece of information (sweep your finger up the edge). What would be the third piece of

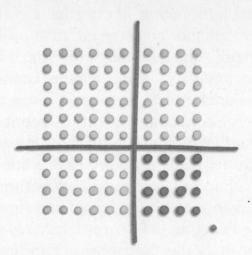

Sixteen divided by four equals four.

information?" The student should sweep a finger along the other edge. Say, "Exactly right, and how many are there?" The student should say, "Four." Say, "Exactly right, and what you just did is called division." Take a good break at this point before proceeding.

Math Exercise 8
Explore Division Using the Grid

The goal here is to get the student to see the simplicity of division as subtracting in groups. We want the student to be able to think with divisions in real quantities, and we also want to prepare him for thinking in quantities of less than a whole one. Again, we will be using the same clay grid.

PROCEDURE

- Remove the ropes and say, "Count over seven and put the rope down." Point to the upper-left (for the student) corner and say, "Beginning here I want you to count out twenty-one. Count to the rope then skip down to the next row, count to the rope and skip down again until you have twenty-one, and put the other rope across." When done, ask, "What are the two pieces of information you have?" The student should indicate the twenty-one in the grid and the seven across the top. Ask, "Where is the third piece of information?" The student should sweep a finger down the side. Ask, "What is the third piece of information?" The student should say, "Three." Say, "What you just did is divide twenty-one by seven." Ask, "Do you see it as that simple?" Look for certainty in the answer.

- Ask, "With what you have there, could you show me where twenty-one divided by three is?" The student should sweep a finger across the top. Ask, "So what is twenty-one divided by three? The student should be able to answer "Seven" without hesitation.

- Ask, "Can you show me twenty divided by five?" If the student says, "Yes," say, "Show me." If the student says, "No," walk him through it as before.

- Continue this process of having the student show you division. Make sure what you ask for are in whole number multiples.

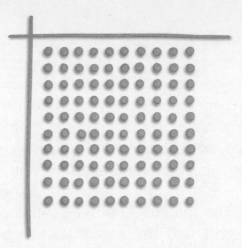

One hundred divided by ten equals ten.

- When you can see the student has certainty, say, "Now the biggest possible division on the grid, show me one hundred divided by ten."

Take a break.

Math Exercise 9
Introduce the Concept of a Quantity
Less Than One

Here, we want to immunize the student against the "deadly fraction disease." Quantities less than an entire single one are a reality, and as such can be easily pictured and manipulated as real objects. Because of this, I think most children by the age of five can already think with the quantity of one-half, but when they hit

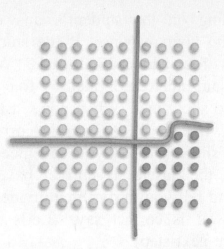

Eighteen divided by four equals four and a half.

fractions in school their ability to think suddenly disappears. We want to make the student comfortable thinking with quantities less than one. We also want to set a foundation that will justify the use of numerals in math, introduce the idea of equal, and pave the way for understanding place value within the numeration system.

PROCEDURE

- Remove the ropes from the grid and say, "Show me eighteen divided by four." The student should count over four and lay the rope down, then when counting out the eighteen, it will be four full rows and only half of the fifth row. Have the student put an "S" bend in the other rope so the entire body of counted balls is contained. Ask, "What's the answer?"

- Depending on the student's answer you must formulate your response. If the student correctly answers, four and one-half, ask, "What would it be if I said nineteen divided by four?" "Move the rope and show me." When done, ask, "So what's the answer?" If the answer is correct, have the student show and tell you seventeen divided by four. If the answer is correct have the student show and tell you thirty-three divided by eight. If the answer is correct say, "Let's do fractions" (skip the next step).

- If the student was not confident in the answer to eighteen divided by four, you can explain the idea of less than one.

- Say, "When you count down this side you are counting the number of rows. We have four complete rows, but this row (point) is not complete. It's not a whole row, so it's not a whole number, it's only a part of a number. To be a whole number there must be four balls in it, but there are only two. So we could say the answer is four full rows and only two of the four balls of the fifth row. That would be a correct answer, but we could make the answer simpler by saying four and two of four. We could make it even simpler by saying four and one-half." Ask, "Do you understand a half?" Regardless of their answer, say, "The idea of a fraction is how much less than a whole one something is. So let's do fractions."

- Move to a different place at the table so the grid isn't between you. From clay, fashion a disk about ¼-inch thick and about two inches in diameter and put it in front of the student. Hand the student the knife and say, "Cut it in half."

- When done, put one piece on top of the other. If they are equal, say, "They are the same, they are equal because equal means the same." Separate the pieces again, and go to the next step.

The concept of the half.

- If they are not reasonably equal say, "It looks like you missed it a bit. To be half the two pieces must be the same, they must be equal. Equal means the same." Fuse the pieces together and have the student cut them again, then place one on top of the other again. Ask, "Are they equal?" Repeat if necessary.

- Put the two pieces of clay touching each other and say, "Cut it in half the other way, so there are four equal pieces." When cut, separate one piece, and ask, "What would this piece be called?" If they say one-fourth, say, "Right." Ask, "Why is it one-fourth?" The answer must be because "It is one of four pieces." If the student doesn't know what it is called or why, you can explain it, and then have the student explain it to you.

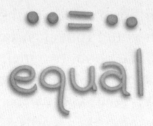

The word equal *defined in clay.*

- Do the same with eighths and sixteenths.

- Finish by doing thirds.

Math Exercise 10
Introduce the Arithmetic Function Symbols

The student needs to recognize the symbols in an equation as telling them what order the equation represents. I want to introduce the concept of doing equations with real numbers so I can introduce numerals.

PROCEDURE
- From clay, fashion an equal sign (=) and ask, "Do you know what this is?" If the student answers correctly, say, "Show me." If there is any hesitation in the answer, explain and demonstrate it, then have the student explain and demonstrate to you.

- From clay, have the student make the word *equal* and go through the Symbol Mastery steps with it.

- Make a plus sign (+) and ask, "Do you know what this is?" If the student answers correctly, say, "Show me." If there is any hesitation in the answer, explain and demonstrate it, then have the student explain and demonstrate to you. Do the Symbol Mastery for words steps outlined in Chapter 15 using the words *add* and *plus*.

- Follow the above model with the minus sign (−) symbol. Do the Symbol Mastery steps using the words *subtract* and *minus*.

- You should now explain and demonstrate the sequence and direction in the equation order. Remember if you are sitting across from the student that your demonstration will be backward from your viewpoint.

- Point to the equal symbol, and say, "There is no direction in this order because it goes in both directions; this side is the same as this side."

- Point to the plus symbol and say, "This sign tells you what to do, but there is no direction or sequence in the order because it is the same if you go in either direction."

- Point to the minus symbol and say, "But this sign not only tells you what to do, it also tells you which direction you must do it." Point and say, "This sign means that you take this many from this many to get this many." "If you go in the other direction you get a different answer, in fact if you go in the wrong direction you get a hole is space and we're not ready yet for holes in space."

- Say, "When we make this kind of thing (sweep your hand over the equation) it is called an *equation;* what we are making is an example of our thinking. In our thinking we know what we are doing to what, but when we are communicating our thinking, we have to show which direction we are going."

- Say, "When we write an equation, whether we do it with a pencil or we do it with clay, we are saying (point) we have this many, we are doing this change to it, with this many. The first piece of information is how many we start with, the sign says what kind of change we are going to make to it, and the second piece of information is how many we are going to make that change with. Of course the answer is always the third piece of information. In the order of an equation we always go in sequence in this direction (point)."

- Have the student explain and demonstrate the direction to you.

- Follow the earlier model with multiplication. When doing the Symbol Mastery use the words *multiply* and *times*.

- Follow the earlier model with division. When doing Symbol Mastery use the words *divide* and *divided by*. Be sure to include the direction here as well.

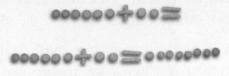

An addition problem and its answer.

A subtraction problem and its answer.

- Play some games with the various arithmetic functions where you make the equation and the student must show the answer. *Example:* Put out six balls, a plus symbol, two balls, and an equal symbol and ask, "How many?" When the student shows you, remove the plus symbol and replace it with a minus symbol. After the student shows the answer, replace the minus symbol with the multiplication symbol, then replace that with the division symbol.

- When the student can win the game every time, say, "Well, you can certainly do arithmetic with real numbers, but what if we had a great big problem like how many days you have been alive times three. Even though you could probably think your way through the problem in a few minutes this way, you could spend the rest of the day making little balls just to show the equation, and all day tomorrow making balls for the answer. Or you could do it with a pencil, and we're back to just a few minutes again."

- Ask, "Are you ready to do math with a pencil?" If the answer is "Yes," go to the next exercise.

- If the answer is no, ask, "What else do you need before you'll be ready?" Provide what the student says is needed.

Math Exercise 11
Introduce Numerals, the Concept of Zero, and the Order of Place Value

The student can now add, subtract, multiply, and divide with real quantities. The next logical step is to learn the same functions symbolically.

PROCEDURE
- Say, "Before we can do math with a pencil there is one more step we must make."

- Make a numeral 2 from clay, and ask, "Do you know what this is?" If the student answers "two" or "the number two," say, "No, this is the *numeral 2*." (Place two balls in front of the student.) Place the numeral so it is above the two balls for the student, and say, "The numeral 2 is a symbol that represents the number two." Point to the two balls and say, "The number and (point to the numeral) the numeral have the same name. The numeral is just a symbol that represents the number."

- Ask, "Does that make sense to you?" If "yes," go on; if "no," continue the explanation.

- Have the student make the numerals 1 through 10 and place them in a row on the table. Point to the 1 and ask, "How many does this numeral represent?" When answered, say, "Show me the number." Have the student put the ball under the numeral.

- Follow the same model with the 2, 3, 4, and 5. Ask, "Could you do this for all the numerals to a 100?" If "yes," go on. If "no," continue until the answer is yes, then go on.

- Point to a place on the table where there is no clay and ask, "How many?" When answered, ask, "Do you know the numeral for zero?" If no, model it for them. Have the student make a 0 and place it before the numeral 1.

- Say, "The zero is very important because without it we cannot do math with a pencil. The idea of zero is there is nothing there, and that is a very important idea."

- Point to the numeral 10 and say, "Show me the number ten." Have the student put the ten balls beneath the numeral.

- Say, "Show me 11." Have the student make the numeral and put the eleven balls under it. Point to

the numeral 11 and say, "You see the numeral 11 is two numeral 1s together. There is a reason for this. The reason is the system that we use goes from nothing to nine, then it repeats again nothing to nine, then it repeats again nothing to nine. It keeps repeating until we have all the numbers there can be. It is called a base ten system because at ten it starts to repeat itself."

- Move to an empty place at the table and say, "Remember the concept of *order*. It is something in its proper place, proper position, and proper condition. We need to create another order to do math with a pencil. It's called *place value*. In this new order we must show the sequence repeating itself."

- Put a numeral 1 on the table and say, "Show me how many."

- When done, put another numeral 1 to the left of the previous one and say, "Show me how many."

- When the student places one ball beneath, point to the two balls and ask, "How many?" The answer is two. Point to the numeral 11 and ask, "What is the name of this numeral?" The answer is eleven.

- Say, "The numeral and the number do not agree; to make them agree we must assign a different order, a new order. In our new order (point to the tens place) this is the place for tens. If there is a numeral 1 here, then there must be the number ten here."

- Say, "Put ten here (point to the single ball in tens place)." When done, ask again, "How many." The answer is eleven.

- Remove the numeral 1 from the ones place and replace it with a 0, and say, "Show and tell me how many."

- When done, replace the zero with the numeral 2, and say, "Show and tell me how many." (12)

- Remove the numeral 1 from the tens place and replace it with a numeral 2, and say, "Show and tell me how many." (22)

- Remove all that has been done. Take a little spot of clay and press it down on the table and say, "Here is the starting point."

- Put a numeral 1 to the student's left of the spot and say, "Show me how many." (1)

- Say, "Count from zero to nine." When done, point to the ones place and say, "This place is their place."

- Place a numeral 1 to the left of the ones place and say, "Show me how many." (11). **Note:** The student need only put a single ball under each one.

- Say, "Count by tens from ten to ninety." When done, point to the tens place and say, "This is the tens place."

- Place a numeral 1 to the left of the tens place and say, "Show me how many." (111). **Note**: The student need only put a single ball under each one.

- Say, "Count by hundreds from one hundred to nine hundred." When done, point to the hundreds place and say, "This is the hundreds place."

- Have the student explain it all to you. When the student has certainty, go on.

- Say, "One last little piece and then we'll need to find a pencil. It's the idea of having less than a whole one, and its place in our new order."

- Point to the ones place and say, "It's less than this so we have to go in this direction (sweep your hand to the right)." Put a numeral one to the right of the spot of clay and say, "Here is where it will go, but is it a ones place or is it a tens place?"

- Point at the ones place and say, "This is the ones place and the smallest whole one we can have is

Introducing decimals.

just one. If we have nine here and we add one more it makes ten (point at the tens place) and it then goes to here."

- Point to the tenths place and say, "So this has to be a tenths place because the least you can have is something cut into two pieces, and we don't have a two's place. If you have one thing and you cut it into ten pieces, if you put the ten pieces back together you will have only one."

- Have the student explain it to you. When done go on.

- Clear a place on the table and roll some strings of clay. Say, "Now we will create the structure for the order for doing math with a pencil."

- Put three balls, a plus symbol, two more balls, an equal symbol, and five balls in a row. Say, "Show me this with numerals." Have the student make a construction with numerals to the left of your construction. When done go on.

- Make a construction with three balls in a row, beneath it (for the student), place a row of two

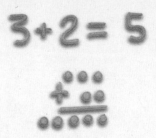

Mathematical notation using clay balls and numerals.

balls and to the left on this row place the plus symbol. Beneath this place a string of clay, and beneath this place five balls.

- Point at the three balls and say, "This is what we start with."

- Point at the plus symbol and say, "This is what kind of change we are going to make to it."

- Point at the two balls and say, "This is what we are going to change it with."

- Point to the string of clay and say, "This is the same as equals."

- Point at the five balls and say, "This is the third piece of information, this is the answer."

- Point at the pieces as you say, "This, changed this way, by this, becomes this."

- Follow the same model for subtraction and multiplication.

- For division, make a division frame and say, "For division this (point at the vertical line) means divide, and this (point at the horizontal line) is the same as equals."

- Put the six balls inside, the two balls in front, and the three balls above. Walk through the process as above.

- Have the student explain it to you.

Take a good break before proceeding.

Math Exercise 12
Teach the Student to Do Arithmetic with a Pencil

The student still needs to learn the art of carrying over, borrowing from, and decimal placement. We want to do the final preparation for the student to be able to go into a math classroom with a word-thinking teacher and be able to function.

PROCEDURE

Addition
- Get out a sheet of paper and the pencil and place them in front of the student.

- Say, "Add 3 to 7." If done correctly, go on.

- Say, "Add 3 to 17." When the student writes the answer, ask, "Did you carry over the numeral 1 from the 10 to the tens place?" **Note**: The student can give the correct answer because he can count.

- If the student doesn't understand your question, walk them through the sequence of addition.

- Say, "7 plus 3 is 10, so the zero goes in the ones place, and the 1 numeral comes over to the tens place, so put the numeral 1 above the numeral 1 in 17. Now add the two together and you get two."

- Explain until the student understands. Then have him explain it to you.

- Say, "Show me 13 added to 27." When correct, go on.

- Say, "Show me 44 added to 66." Watch to see that the student carries a numeral 1 from the ones place to the tens place, and that a numeral 1 is carried over from the tens place to the hundreds place. Continue until the student has certainty on carrying over.

- Say, "Show me 3.5 (three-point-five) added to 5.125 (five-point-one-two-five)." Watch how the student draws the problem.

- If not drawn correctly, wait until the student answers, and say, "The addition was correct but the place in the order was wrong so the answer is not correct. When you draw the problem with the

$$3.5$$
$$5.125$$
$$\overline{8.625}$$

How the problem should look on paper.

pencil you must create the proper order. In the proper order the ones place numerals must line up. It's easy to remember that the decimal points must always line up."

- Say, "Show me 3.5 (three-point-five) added to 5.125 (five-point-one-two-five) drawn in its proper order." If not correct, give additional instructions.

- When drawn correctly, ask for the answer. If correct, go on.

- Do decimal fraction addition until the student has certainty.

- Finish by having the student add 99.5 (ninety-nine-point-five) to 999.5 (nine-hundred-ninety-nine-point-five).

Subtraction
- Replace the sheet of paper and say, "Subtract 7 from 9." Instruct if not correct. When correct, go on.

- Say, "Subtract 7 from 13." When correct, go on.

- Say, "Subtract 7 from 23." When the students writes the answer, ask, "Did you borrow a numeral 1 from the numeral 2 in the tens place?" **Note:** the student can answer because he can count backward from 23.

- If the student doesn't understand, walk him through the subtraction, showing how to borrow 1 from the 2 in the tens place. Put a strike through the numeral 2 to show it has been reduced by a quantity of 10. When the student has got the concept, go on.

- Say, "Show me 16 subtracted from 44." Watch to see that the borrowing steps are done correctly. Continue until the student has certainty on borrowing.

- Say, "Show me 9.5 (nine-point-five) subtracted from 15." Watch to see that the student draws the problem correctly.

- If drawn correctly, say, "Very good, you've drawn the proper order."

- If not drawn correctly, wait until the student answers and say, "The subtraction was correct but the place in the order was wrong so the answer is not correct. When you draw the problem with the pencil you must create the proper order. In the proper order the ones place numerals must line up. It's easy to remember that the decimal points must always line up."

- Say, "Show me 9.5 (nine-point-five) subtracted from 15 drawn in its proper order." If not correct give additional instructions. When drawn correctly, ask for the answer. If correct, go on.

- Do decimal fraction subtraction until the student has certainty.

- Finish by having the student subtract 98.5 (ninety-eight-point-five) from 100.

Multiplication

- Replace the sheet of paper and say, "Multiply 7 by 3." If done correctly, go on.

- Say, "Multiply 17 by 3." If the student has any difficulty, walk him through it. Say, "7 times 3 is 21, the numeral 1 goes in the ones place, the numeral 2 carries over to the tens place to be added later. 3 times 1 is 3, plus the 2 that were carried over is 5, so the numeral 5 goes in the tens place. The third piece of information is 51." Explain as necessary until the student gets the idea, then go on.

- Say, "Show me 5 times 12." Walk through and explain if necessary, then go on.

- Say, "Show me 11 times 22." Watch to see that the student is drawing the numerals in their proper place-value place. If not drawn correctly, wait until the student answers and say, "When you are working out the answer you must draw it in a way to maintain its proper order. The place value of the numerals must be maintained. The ones place numerals must line up, and the tens place numerals must line up so you can add them correctly. Because the order was wrong the answer is not correct. When you draw the problem with the pencil you must create and maintain the proper order. In the proper order the ones place numerals must line up, and the tens place, and so on."

- Walk the student through the problem by asking, "Is it a ones place, tens place, or hundreds place numeral?" When answered, say, "So draw it where it should go."

- Say, "Show me 55 times 125."

- Continue this kind of exercise until the student has certainty on doing multiplication with a pencil, then go on.

- Say, "Show me 3.5 (three-point-five) times 5.25 (five-point-two-five)."

- Instruct as necessary.

- Continue decimal fraction multiplication until the student has certainty, then go on.

Division

- Replace the sheet of paper and say, "Because you can multiply with a pencil, and you can subtract with a pencil, you already know how to divide with a pencil. You only need to know how it is ordered and in what sequence you do things in."

• Say, "Sometimes when you have a division problem you have to estimate, in other words you have to make a guess. When this occurs, the best thing to do is what I call 'best guess, try and see.' If your guess isn't correct, your pencil has an eraser on it, so you can always fix it. Don't let the uncertainty of making a guess scare you away. If you come up with the right answer in the end, it doesn't matter how many times you had to guess along the way."

• Say, "Divide 15 by 5." If correct, go on. **Note**: Because the student may be able to think with the grid they may be able to answer the problem without actually going through the steps. You must do division that is beyond the limit of the grid.

• Say, "Divide 134 by 12." Watch how the student draws the problem and the sequence of the manipulations. Instruct as necessary.

• After each instruction have the student instruct you with the explanation of why the particular placement is made or sequence is followed.

• Continue doing examples until the student has certainty as to the proper order and sequence, then go on.

- Say, "Divide 7.5 (seven-point-five) by 5." Watch the placement of the decimal point and instruct as necessary.

- Say, "Next we are going to divide 150 by 2.5 (two-point-five), but before you start there is a trick you should know about the decimal point. Draw the framework for 150, divided by 2.5, and I'll show you the trick."

- When drawn, say, "I have asked you to divide with a number that isn't a whole number. That decimal fraction on the end can really mess things up, so the first step in the sequence is to change the order of the decimal placement. It is really easy to do with the pencil. You can move the numeral five from the tenths position to the ones position by moving the decimal over one place. You can get away with this trick only if you also move the decimal over one position in the number that you are dividing into. You can move the decimal point over as many places as you need to as long as you also move it the same number of places for both sets of numerals."

- Have the student add a decimal point to 150, and place a 0 in the tenths place. Then, have the student put the caret mark changing the 2.5 to 25.

- Say, "Now you must also add the caret mark changing 150 to 1,500 (one thousand five hundred). Now do what you already know how to do and you'll get the answer."

$$2.5\overline{)150}$$

$$2.5_\wedge\overline{)150.0_\wedge}$$

Decimal place movement.

- Do additional exercises dividing by fractional numbers until the student has certainty.

- When the student can do three-place division, with fractional quantities, using numerals, with certainty, your job is finished.

SECTION FIVE

Addressing Handwriting

Agraphia and Dysgraphia

CHAPTER 20

A Correction Strategy for Handwriting Problems

In Chapter 5, we listed seven possible causes for handwriting problems. We believe that four of those seven problems can be addressed and corrected. They occur as a result of:

- no or inadequate instruction,

- disorientation,

- multiple mental images, and

- inadequate natural orientation.

The underlying strategy is the simple truth that *if you eliminate the reason a problem exists, the problem will cease to exist.* Once you determine the cause, you will be able to directly address the problem and correct it using the tools in the following chapters.

Because handwriting is an art form that requires learning specific skills, just eliminating the reason the skills weren't developed in the first place will not magically give someone appropriate handwriting. After you eliminate the underlying reason, your student will still need to learn the skills. Once the student is capable of developing them, you'll need to provide adequate instructions.

With the proper understanding and the proper tools, you will attack the problem step-by-step. Some problems will require more steps than others, but all you need to do is take one step at a time in the proper sequence.

Install the Basic Tools

Some basic steps and procedures are appropriate for all these handwriting categories. The first step is to properly motivate your student. Follow the information in Chapter 7, "Motivation and Responsibility," to get your student properly motivated. How would your student benefit from being able to write comfortably and legibly?

The common thread running through all four of these handwriting problem areas is disorientation. Therefore, you must address this before you can do anything else. Addressing it at this stage will provide a foundation for later work in any problem category.

The first step is to give the student a tool—a procedure to use—which will allow him to be mentally present with you. The student must experience the same real-world environment. This requires being oriented. First, perform the Perceptual Ability Assessment exercise in Chapter 8 to help you determine which of the two orientation methods to use. There are two such tools to choose from: Alignment, in Chapter 12, and Davis Orientation Counseling, in Chapter 9. Once you decide which to use, follow the appropriate procedure as directed.

Once your student can become oriented, he will need some additional tools to make it comfortable for him to remain oriented and reorient at will. Chapter 10, Release and Review for Orientation Counseling, will allow him to let go of any feelings of stress and tension. And the Dial Setting procedure in Chapter 13, will allow him to adjust his energy level and the speed of his internal clock.

Once your student has these tools, you can address his particular handwriting problem. You may have already spotted the problem category of your student. If so, skip to the chapter that describes how to deal with that category for the checklist and the rest of the word map.

If you haven't yet determined the category of your student's problem, evaluate it based upon the information in Chapter 5. If your student seems to fit into more than one category, address the more severe one first. They are listed in order of increasing severity: *Inadequate instruction* is the least severe, and *inadequate natural orientation* is the most severe.

A word of caution: If you attempt to apply the procedures for a category that doesn't fit your student, you may hit a solid brick wall. If that happens, stop and reevaluate. Once you have chosen the correct category, your student should begin to make noticeable progress from the very beginning.

CHAPTER 21

Handwriting Correction for No or Inadequate Instruction

The problem here is that the student never acquired the skills necessary for handwriting. The reason the skills are missing is simply that little if any effective instruction was provided to the student. As I said previously, something may have blocked the development of these skills. If so, the block must be removed before you address the missing skills. The purpose of these exercises is to guide a picture-thinking student past the pitfalls that would prevent him from developing writing skills.

These problems can range from minor to severe. At one end of the spectrum, a student might just have difficulty making the transition from block printing to cursive handwriting. At the other end, he might not even be able to hold and manipulate a writing instrument. What follows is the worst-case scenario, so your student may not need to do every step. Just select those that seem relevant to your student's needs. Once the student can easily do what is required in any step, consider it finished and go on to the next exercise.

As an adult dyslexic, my major problem was in

deciphering the written language. It's logical that if I couldn't read it, I wouldn't be able to write it. Therefore, it shouldn't be surprising that I also manifested the symptoms of dysgraphia. With the development of the Davis Dyslexia Correction Procedures I managed to resolve the deciphering problem. With that, my writing began to improve without any instruction or effort on my part. Whatever instruction I received in school didn't "take" because I hadn't learned to achieve an oriented state. The old me would only write something when there was absolutely no way to avoid it. When I wrote, I actually printed in uppercase letters only, with the first letter of each word larger than the others. It took all of the effort and concentration I could muster just to get the words to go straight across the page, even on lined paper. My writing was done in three stages: First I would get the ideas scribbled down on a piece of paper. Then I would look up the spelling for each word in the dictionary. The final stage was to print the properly spelled words straight across the page. The only thing I could write in cursive style was my name. Even after my handwriting (block printing) began to improve, I still lacked many skills needed for handwriting. I enlisted the aid of Dr. Fatima Ali to help, and the model she provided me was the foundation for the one I'm now sharing with you.

Preparation and Procedure

I recommend that your student master the alphabet as described in Chapter 15. If there is any doubt or confusion associated with any of the individual characters, it could interfere with learning handwriting skills.

INSTALL THE BASIC TOOLS
The basic tool package should already be in place, as described in the previous chapter. The student should have a means of controlling his orientation, a method of releasing tension and stress, and a method of controlling his energy level and the speed of his internal clock.

MATERIALS NEEDED
1. Writing form models.

- If your student is attending school, the writing examples should be in the school's approved writing form. If the school can't provide them, they should be available from a local teacher/ school supply store.
- Use the same examples throughout the following procedures. If you need additional copies, get them from the same source or make photocopies of an original.
- If your student is no longer in school, writing examples should be available from a teacher/ school supply store. We recommend the workbook, *Cursive Connections,* by Kathryn Libby, which is briefly described in the back of this book.

2. Three-lined, beginning writing practice tablets (available at most stationery stores or teacher/school

supply stores). NOTE: Make sure that the line spacing of the writing form models and the three-lined practice tablets are the same.

3. Tracing paper.

4. An assortment of soft lead pencils.

5. A pencil sharpener.

6. Age-appropriate reading material.

7. A ruler.

8. A common notepad tablet with wide spaces (about half an inch).

Correction Procedure

The exercise is done in four progressive phases:

Phase 1, *Tracing,* provides the student with two important aspects of the art form. It introduces the forms and shapes of the letters to the student's picture-thinking process. And it begins the development of fine motor skills (muscle coordination).

Phase 2, *Copying,* requires the student to use mental imagery to create the forms and shapes of the letters. And it furthers the development of muscle coordination.

Phase 3, *Originating,* furthers the use of mental imagery and builds muscle coordination. The student assembles various letter combinations without models to follow.

Phase 4, *Conversion,* allows the student to make the

switch from practice paper to standard notepad paper, and to exercise and practice the new skills.

As you go through these exercises, always maintain good communication with the student. Take frequent breaks. It's better to take too many than not enough.

PHASE 1: TRACING

Preparation: Set up your work space, have the student sit directly across the table from you, then perform the following steps:

- Have the student check orientation. If the student uses the Alignment procedure, say "Feel your imaginary hands on your shoulders." If the student uses the Orientation procedure, say "Check your point."

- Have the student do Release.

- Have the student set his Energy Dial to an appropriate setting for this activity.

- Give the student an explanation of what you expect, in language appropriate to the student's age. Example: "We are going to master handwriting. We will be using your gifts and your artistic ability to do it. If you just do what I ask you to do it will be easy."

- Give the student instructions on holding the pencil. Have the student hold a pencil the way he would when he writes something. If the grip is adequate, go on. If not, model holding the pencil and ask the student to hold the pencil the same way you're holding it. You may need to have the student do Release again to make it comfortable to change his grip. You may also need to help by placing his fingers correctly on the pencil.

- Have the student adjust the firmness of his grip on the pencil. Ask him to practice putting the feeling of Release into his hand and fingers. I have often asked my students to hold the pencil as if they were holding a tiny baby bird. Say, "Hold the pencil just like it's a baby bird. You need to hold it tight enough that it can't get away, but loose enough not to squash it." Then, if you see the grip becoming tight or the pressure on the paper becoming too heavy, you can caution the student while he is writing by saying, "Oh, you're squashing the bird!"

- Check to make sure the student's feet are on the floor. You may need to find a footstool or something equivalent. Good posture for writing begins with the feet on a solid foundation.

Procedure: Now you're ready to begin the exercise. Place the writing example and a pencil on the table in front of the student. Cover the writing example with a sheet of tracing paper.

1. Point at the first letter example on the sheet and say, "Trace this letter exactly." Observe the student: If his posture slumps, stop him, have him check orientation, reset the dial and do Release, then let him continue. If the student is using too much pencil pressure or the pencil grip tightens, stop him, have him do Release, then let him continue. Posture is important. Leaning forward or resting the other hand isn't necessarily poor posture, but curling up over the work is. Do not overuse the instructions. If the student slumps every time he begins, suggest letting his orientation hold him upright as he works.

2. When the student has finished, check to see if the tracing is exact. If it isn't exact, say, "That's pretty good." Slide the tracing paper slightly sideways so a blank space is over the same letter and say, "Try it again." Continue until it is an exact copy of the printed letter below.

3. If it is exact, or when it finally is, say, "Excellent!" Have the student check Orientation, Release, Dial Setting, and pencil grip. If he needs a break, take one.

4. Move the tracing paper so the previously drawn letters don't interfere. Point to the next letter and say, "Trace this letter exactly." Repeat steps 1 through 3 on the next letter.

5. Repeat these steps for the entire alphabet, using both upper and lowercase characters. Do not have the student trace any letter combinations yet, only the individual letters.

6. Finally, have the student make a "master" tracing of all the letter shapes on a single sheet of tracing paper, with all the characters traced exactly. When this is complete, go on to Phase 2.

PHASE 2: COPYING

Preparation: Follow the same format as Phase 1.

Procedure: Place the writing example, practice tablet, and a pencil on the table in front of the student. Check to be sure the practice tablet spacing is the same size as the writing example. Have the student's master tracing handy.

1. Point at the first letter and say, "Make a copy of this letter." Point to a line on the practice tablet and say, "Here." Observe the student: If his posture slumps, stop him and have him check orientation, reset his dial, and do Release. Then let him continue. If the student is using too much pencil pressure or the pencil grip tightens, stop him and have him do Release, then let him continue.

2. When the student has finished say, "That's pretty good. Put your master tracing over it and see if it's exact." Have the student do so.

3. If it isn't exact, ask, "How is it different?" or "What would you have to do to make it better?"

4. Have the student remove the tracing and say, "Try it again."

5. Have the student put the master tracing over the letter again and check the exactness of the copy. If it isn't exact, repeat steps 3 and 4.

6. If it is exact, or when it finally is, say, "Excellent!"

7. Have the student draw a full line of the same letter across the page on the practice tablet.

8. Have the student do steps 1 through 7 on the rest of the letters.

9. Have the student do steps 1 through 7 on letter combinations from the writings.

10. When complete, go on.

PHASE 3: ORIGINATING
Preparation: Follow the same format as Phase 1.
Procedure: Place the writing example, practice tablet, and a pencil on the table in front of the student. Have the student's master tracing and some age-appropriate reading material handy. From the reading material,

Have the student check each letter using the master tracing, then draw a full line of letters on the practice pad.

select a short, simple sentence, and give the student this instruction:

1. Point to a line on the tablet and say, "Write the word *[first word of the sentence]* here." Observe the student's posture and pencil grip as in phases 1 and 2.

2. Have the student evaluate the correctness of the written letters. If necessary, have the student repeat the step.

3. Repeat step 1 with the next word of the sentence. If the first word was satisfactory to the student, the next word can go next to it. If the first word was not satisfactory, the next word should go below on its own line.

4. Have the student evaluate the correctness of the written letters. If necessary, have the student repeat the step.

5. Continue repeating step 1 using all the words of the sentence.

6. If any of the words were written on separate lines, have the student write all the words next to each other on one line as a complete sentence.

7. If necessary, instruct the student on spacing between words (enough to fit an additional letter).

8. If necessary, have the student write the sentence again with proper spacing.

9. If you choose to, you can instruct the student on spelling, capitalization, and punctuation as they apply to handwriting. But teaching grammar should be done separately.

10. Have the student write another sentence from the reading material. Gauge your interactions to the needs of the student.

11. Continue as above with additional sentences. Continue practicing until the student is proficient.

PHASE 4: CONVERTING

Preparation: Follow the same format as Phase 1.
Procedure: Place the notepad, the three-lined practice tablet, and a pencil on the table in front of the student.

Have the ruler, tracing paper, and sentence examples from Phase 3 close at hand.

1. Have the student compare the three-lined practice tablet and the notepad. He must notice that it isn't just the dotted line that is missing, but also the space above and below the lines. The notepad really isn't two-lined; it is single-lined. In order for the student to convert to using it, he must mentally imagine the two additional lines in order for his spacing to be correct. Conversationally, discuss how the lines are laid out until the student realizes that the single space between the lines must be divided into three spaces in order to make the regular tablet match the practice tablet.

2. Take the notepad and use the ruler to draw in the two missing lines in the top three spaces. You will have to estimate dividing the spaces into thirds. (The actual measurement of the space between lines is $11/32$ of an inch, so it can't be measured with a regular ruler.) So start by making two equally spaced dots between the printed lines at each side of the page. Then connect the dots using the ruler. You may need to practice this.

3. Pass the notepad to the student and ask him to write one of the sentences he wrote earlier, using the lines you just drew in. The challenge is to reduce the size of the letters to fit the new, smaller spacing. If the sentence selected doesn't fill the three lines with text, have the student continue writing the same

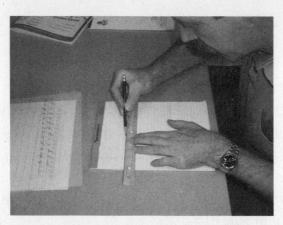

You'll need to draw in two extra lines so the standard writing tablet matches the practice pad.

sentence over again until all three lines are complete. If necessary, repeat this step until the student has successfully adjusted to writing smaller.

4. Have the student divide the following three spaces into thirds with the ruler as you did earlier. Then have him write another one of the sentences he wrote earlier in the spaces he just drew in. As before, have the student fill the entire three lines with text.

5. Have the student divide the following space with the ruler, then skip the next space, and then divide the following one. Have the student write another one of the sentences. When he gets to the undivided line; say, "Imagine the lines are there and write using the imaginary lines." Have the student fill all three lines with text. Ask the student to evaluate how well he did on the undivided line.

Your student needs to mentally fill in the two extra lines that were on the practice pad.

6. Take a piece of tracing paper and use the ruler to trace a four-line set (two printed lines with two added lines between) from a set of lines that were drawn on the notepad tablet earlier. The tracing paper lines will be placed over the student's handwriting for evaluation.

7. Have the student write sentences on more undivided lines, using his imagination for dividing the spaces. He can check his accuracy using the tracing paper lines. Continue this step until the student can write an undivided line of text that is adequately sized.

When the student can comfortably and confidently write text in an appropriate size on the undivided spaces of the tablet, he no longer needs your help. Congratulations!

CHAPTER 22

Handwriting Correction
for Disorientation

Two different handwriting problems fall within this category. The most common is "dysgraphia," which often accompanies reading dyslexia. I define it as *disorientation that is stimulated by the act or process of writing.* Before you begin, if you haven't already, do a quick check for reading dyslexia. Simply have the student read a paragraph aloud to you from something that is appropriate to his grade level. If he leaves out or misreads more than one of the small "trigger words"—such as *the, and, a, an, for, at,* and *of*—or loses his place, or skips a line, or ignores the punctuation, those are all signs of reading dyslexia.

You should also check his understanding or comprehension, even if he appears to read the material flawlessly. If the student can't tell you the main points of the paragraph, he probably has a reading problem that causes the writing problem.

The full correction procedures for reading dyslexia are contained in the book *The Gift of Dyslexia.* In almost all cases where reading dyslexia is accompanied by dysgraphia, once the reading problems are corrected, the dysgraphia simply disappears. If it doesn't, the student only needs to be guided through the procedures in Chapter 21, "Handwriting Correction for No or Inadequate Instruction."

The second problem category, where the handwriting problem itself is caused by disorientation, is the one we will address here. This category is rare in children to begin with, and you're unlikely to see it accompanied by reading dyslexia.

The anatomy of this problem category is that there is a trigger—a line, shape, or motion—that produces an emotion, which in turn causes disorientation. These emotions actually come from the individual's life experiences. Somewhere in the past is a real experience that produced the emotion. Somehow a line drawn in a particular direction, or of a certain shape, or using a particular motion reminds the individual of the experience. Subconsciously linking the line, shape, or motion to the past experience brings the emotion forward in time. The person begins to experience the past emotion in the present, and the result is a disorientation.

At the exact point where the disorientation appears, the person will make a "glitch" in his handwriting. By that, I mean an involuntary jerk or twitch that shows up in the line being drawn.

Preparation and Procedure

After following the instructions mapped out in Chapter 20, the basic tool package should be in place. The person should have a means of controlling his disorientation, a method of releasing tension and stress, and a method of controlling his energy level and the speed of his internal clock. You will need the following materials:

- lined writing paper

- an easel with a large pad of flip-chart paper

- various writing instruments such as pens or pencils, plus a marker

The goal is to find and eliminate the triggers for disorientation. It seldom takes more than an hour or two. Finding the triggers is easy, but eliminating them can be a bit more difficult. Triggers can be eliminated in two ways:

1. The trigger can be desensitized. In an oriented state, the student repetitively encounters the stimulus, making the same line, shape, or motion over and over. Each encounter removes some of the intensity of the emotion that is being stimulated by the trigger. Continued encounters will eventually result in the student feeling nothing as a result of the encounter. At that point the link between the line, shape, or motion and the past experience is broken. The stimulus has been eliminated.

2. The time link between the past emotional experience and "now" can be broken by identifying the emotion itself. In an oriented state, the student repetitively encounters the stimulus. As the student describes what is being felt, sooner or later the images of the past experience will become visible to the student. Asking the student to describe the past experience in the "now" will break the time link. This may require many repetitions, but once the link is broken, the line, shape, or motion will no longer cause the disorienting emotion.

PREPARATION

- Have the student sit across the table from you.

- Have the student check orientation. For the Alignment procedure say, "Feel your imaginary hands on your shoulders," or for Orientation say, "Check your point."

- Have the student do Release.

- Ask the student to set his Energy Dial to an appropriate setting for this activity.

- Give the student an explanation of what you expect, in language appropriate to the student's age. Example: "We're going to find and eliminate the triggers that are causing this writing problem. What actually causes the disorientation is what you are feeling, so we are looking for what you are feeling at the exact moment the disorientation happens. So when I ask, 'What are you feeling?' I'm asking about the change in feeling you just had. I'm asking about your emotion."

FIND THE HANDWRITING GLITCHES AND TRIGGERS

Place the lined paper pad and a pencil on the table in front of the student.

- Tell the student to write the sentence, "The quick brown fox jumped over the sleeping dog's back. Then sign your name at the end of it." If the student has written the sentence in micro-writing, as described in Chapter 5, instruct him to write the sentence again making the words as large as possible while staying within the lines.

  Note: The probable reason for micro-writing is that it minimizes the student's encounter with the stimulus. Tiny handwriting also makes it difficult for you to spot a trigger. The writing must be large enough for you to detect a "glitch"—a misshapen line, either straight or curved, that forms or connects the letters in the student's writing.

- Observe the student. Watch for the point where a glitch appears in the handwriting. That's the point of disorientation. Be aware of the student's frustration level. Don't let him struggle too much.

- Once the student has finished the sentence, assess the writing, looking for glitches. You'll see the

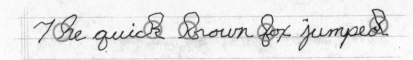

A typical repetitive "glitch" where the student can't draw a continuous loop when forming letters.

same glitch in every place where the student made the same motion to write that type of line or shape. Usually you will find only one type, but not always, so check to see if there are more.

Important Note: If the glitch appears only in the student's signature, but not anywhere else, stop the instruction. This indicates a psychological problem with the person's identity or self-image that will require a professional therapist to address.

- Once you find a glitch, determine whether the stimulus is the motion itself, or the student's reaction to a particular line or shape that is being drawn on the paper. The motion stimulus requires a different approach than the others.

- To check for a motion trigger, have the student exaggerate the movement used to draw the line or shape where the glitch occurred. Do this by asking the student to slowly swing his arm and hand through the motion in the air in front of him, as if drawing a giant-sized letter in the air.

- At the point in the movement where the glitch would appear on the paper ask, "What do you feel right there?" If the student doesn't feel any emotion, have him repeat the swinging motion two or three more times, repeating the question, "What do you feel?" If the student doesn't detect any feeling in the movement skip to Eliminating Line and Shape Triggers, below.

ELIMINATING MOTION TRIGGERS

If the student noticed some sensation while making the movement, ask him to describe what he felt. He will probably describe a physical feeling something like, "A cold chill up my back," or "A wave of nausea." Then ask, "What emotion would come with that feeling?" Note what the student says.

- Have the student recheck orientation. ("Feel your imaginary hands on your shoulders," or "Check your point.")

- Have him repeat the exaggerated motion. Again at the appropriate point in the motion ask, "What do you feel?" If the student gives a sensation instead of an emotion, ask, "What emotion would come with that feeling?" Note what he says. You're after the emotion. There are several different possible responses:

(a) If the student gives a different emotion then the one described previously, repeat the steps of checking orientation and performing the exaggerated motion until the emotion felt is consistent.

(b) If or when the student gives the same emotion, ask, "Was it more intense or less intense the last time?" If less intense, continue repeating the steps of checking orientation and making the exaggerated motion until the student "feels nothing" while performing the motion. (The trigger may desensitize at any point during this procedure, so you may be finished. If so, skip to the last instruction in this sequence.)

(c) If the emotion is more intense, repeat the steps of checking orientation and making the exaggerated motion again. Then ask, "Was it more intense or less intense this time?" If less intense, follow (a) above. If more intense ask; "What mental images do you get with that emotion?" The student may or may not be able to tell you. If he does tell you, make a note of it. **Note:** Do not have the student do Release or reset his Energy Dial at this point. You don't want the student to break contact with the past experience.

• Repeat step (b). Again there are two possibilities: Linking the emotion to the images may suddenly break the time link so the motion no longer comes forward in time. Or, as the student describes the images, he may begin to vent the emotion. The venting can bring tears and a disorientation into the past experience (the student reexperiences it mentally). If this occurs, you must let it run its course.

- Continue repeating step (b) until the time link breaks. Once it does, the emotional link also breaks. The student will not exhibit the emotion. This is usually accompanied by a smile and an "in the now" comment.

- Whatever the student says, simply say, "That would explain it." Have the student check orientation, do Release, and repeat the exaggerated motion. It should cause no feeling.

- Take a short break.

- Have the student write the sentence, "The quick brown fox jumped over the sleeping dog's back" again. Assess again for glitches. If there are additional glitches, select one and work with it following the same procedure as above. When the glitches are gone, this job is finished.

ELIMINATING LINE AND SHAPE TRIGGERS

If the student didn't notice any sensation while making the exaggerated arm movement, the problem is a line or shape trigger. These are both addressed in the same way.

Writing large with a marker on a vertical plane
may help reveal "glitches."

- On the flip chart, have the student use the marker to write (very large) a word from the previous sentence that contained a glitch. If the glitch doesn't show up with the flip chart in the vertical plane, lay the pad on the table and have the student write the word in the horizontal plane. **Note:** When the student writes larger, the glitch may not be larger than in normal size writing, so you may see large writing with little tiny glitches. These can be difficult to detect. Even so, the student's contact with the stimulus is longer when drawing larger lines and shapes. Usually the glitches will appear in only one type of line or shape, but not always. If you find more than one type, deal with each one sequentially as they show up.

- Assess the written word for the glitches. Select a segment of a line or a shape that contains a glitch. This might be only a quarter of a letter or a stroke that contains the glitch in its middle.

- Have the student redraw just that segment. At the point where the glitch occurred ask, "What do you feel?" As with motion triggers, he may respond with something like, "A cold chill up my back," or "A wave of nausea." Ask, "What emotion would come with that feeling?" Note what the student says.

  1. Have the student recheck orientation. ("Feel your imaginary hands on your shoulders," or "Check your point.")

  2. Have the student draw the segment again. When he comes to the point in the stroke where the glitch was, ask, "What do you feel?" If the student gives a sensation instead of an emotion, ask, "What emotion would come with that feeling?" Note what is said. You're after the emotion. There are several different possible responses.

     (a) If the student gives a different emotion, repeat the steps of checking orientation and drawing the segment until the emotion is consistent.

     (b) If, or when, the student gives the same emotion, ask, "Was it more intense or less intense this time?"

i. If less intense, continue repeating the steps of checking orientation and drawing the segment until the student "feels nothing" while drawing the segment. (You may be finished here. Skip to the last instruction in this sequence.)

ii. If more intense, repeat the steps of checking orientation and drawing the segment again, then ask, "Was it more intense or less intense this time?" If less intense follow (i) above. If more intense, ask, "What images do you get with that emotion?" The student may or may not be able to tell you. If the student tells you, make a note of it.

- Repeat step (ii). Again there are two possibilities: Linking the emotion to the images may suddenly break the time link, and the motion will no longer come forward in time. Or, as the student is describing the images, he will begin to vent the emotion. The venting can bring tears and an apparent disorientation into the past experience (the student reexperiences it mentally). If this occurs, you must let it run its course.

- Continue repeating step (ii) until the time link breaks. When it does, the emotional link also breaks, so the student will no longer exhibit the emotion. It's usually accompanied by a smile and an "in the now" comment.

- Whatever the student says, simply say, "That would explain it." Have the student check orientation, do Release, and repeat the exaggerated motion. There should be no feeling.

- Take a short break.

- Have the student write the sentence, "The quick brown fox jumped over the sleeping dog's back" again. Assess once more for glitches. If more show up, begin again with one of them. When no more glitches show up, you are finished.

Our job is twofold: First we must find and identify the trigger, and then we must eliminate it. If there are more than one, they can be eliminated one at a time.

If for some reason the previous procedures did not alleviate the handwriting problem or induced some negative effect in your student, you should refer your student to a trained licensed psychologist or therapist for additional treatment.

CHAPTER 23

Handwriting Correction for Multiple Mental Images

This problem exists because the student has multiple mental images of what writing *should* look like. The instructions below will help you assist the student in eliminating the multiple images and replacing them with single, simple, accurate images.

Preparation and Procedure

If you haven't done so already, install the basic tools package in Part II. The student should have a means of controlling disorientation, a method of releasing tension and stress, and a method of controlling his energy level and the speed of his internal clock. To complete the exercise, you will need: a lined paper pad, six or more pencils, and a pencil sharpener.

PREPARATION
- Have the student sit across the table from you.

- Have the student check orientation: If the student uses the Alignment procedure, say, "Feel your imaginary hands on your shoulders." If the student uses the Orientation procedure, say, "Check your point."

- Have the student do Release.

- Have the student set his Energy Dial to an appropriate level for this activity.

- Give the student an explanation of what you expect. Your explanation must be in language appropriate for the student's age. Example: "We are going to be solving a problem by erasing the reason the problem is there in the first place. We will be using a part of your gift to get rid of the problem. You will be erasing some mental pictures. Do you know what a mental picture is?"

- If the student can't tell you what a mental picture is walk him through a simple demonstration like, "Have you ever seen a lion?" He may say only on TV or in the movies or yes. (If "no" use a cat or dog, but you need a "yes" answer). Ask him to describe a lion. Before he finishes the description ask, "Are you looking at a lion?" The answer should be "yes"—I have never experienced a student saying "no" to this, but if I did I would ask the student to "imagine" the lion he just described. Say, "You're not looking at the lion with your eyes are you? Your mind's eye is looking at a picture of a lion. That picture is a mental image. A mental image is a picture that your mind's eye can see."

- Give the student instructions on holding the pencil. Ask him to grip a pencil as he would normally hold it to write something. If the pencil grip is adequate, go on. If not, model holding a pencil by asking the student to hold the pencil the way you do. You may need to have him do the Release procedure again to make it easier for him to change his grip. You may also need to help by placing his fingers appropriately on the pencil.

- Have the student adjust the firmness of his grip on the pencil. Ask him to "put the feeling of release" into his hand and fingers. If the student grips the pencil too tightly, I always use the ploy of likening the pencil to a baby bird. I say, "Hold the pencil just like it's a baby bird. You need to hold it tight enough that it can't get away, but loose enough not to squash it." Then, as the student is writing, if the grip tightens or the pressure on the paper is too much, I caution the student by saying "Oh, you're squashing the bird!"

PROCEDURE

- Place the paper and a pencil on the table in front of the student. Point at a line on the paper and say, "On this line, write *[student's first name]* is good." The only purpose in doing this step is to have the student access his mental images. The student must be in contact with the mental images for the erasing step.

- Observe the student. If his posture slumps, stop him and have him reset his Energy Dial and do Release, then let him continue. *Do not* have him check orientation or reorient at this point. If he is using too mush pencil pressure, or his pencil grip tightens, stop him and have him do Release, then continue. *Do not* have him reorient or check orientation. This will break his contact with the mental images and prevent the procedure from working! Be aware of the student's frustration level. Don't let him struggle too much. Keep in mind that you have asked him to do something he cannot do. If you see him struggling too hard say, "That's good for now" and stop him before he finishes.

- Just as the student finishes writing the phrase or you have stopped him, immediately ask, *"Do you have any mental pictures of what writing should look like?"* Do not alter the wording. An alternate wording could undermine the effectiveness of the procedure. If need be, you can explain what a mental picture is. You must ask this question quickly before the student's attention shifts to something else. You want to do it while the student is still in contact with the mental images.

- If the student replies yes, say, "Erase them and tell me when they are gone." When the student says they are gone, have him recheck orientation. (For Alignment, "Feel your imaginary hands on your shoulders." Or for Orientation, "Check your point.") If the student replies no, make sure he understands the concept of mental pictures. Then have the student write the same sentence again and ask the question before he has finished writing the sentence. If he doesn't find mental pictures of what handwriting should look like after a few tries, this probably wasn't the problem in the first place.

- Assess the student's emotional state and stress level: If the student would benefit from doing the Release, have him do it. If the student would benefit from a change in energy level or his sense of time, have him reset his Energy Dial. If the student would benefit from taking a break, take one.

- Repeat the instruction steps. The procedure for eliminating multiple mental images is completed by many repetitions, erasing more images each time. When the student says he has no more mental pictures of what writing should look like, this part of the procedure is complete. The student no longer has multiple overlaid mental images that

interfere with writing. The reason he couldn't learn and develop handwriting skills has been eliminated. A major goal has been attained!

However, this is not an end but a new beginning. A student who had this problem still won't have the fine motor skills needed for handwriting in cursive style. So now it's time to go through the procedures for No or Inadequate Instruction in Chapter 21.

A few students may have difficulty with those instructions. If your student does, try these two preliminary steps. They should make things easier.

- Follow the procedures for mastering the upper- and lowercase alphabet as outlined in Chapter 15.

- Have the student model the cursive alphabet letters in clay, in both upper- and lowercase.

When your student has completed the procedures outlined in the Chapter 21, your work with the student is complete.

HELPFUL HINTS

Here are some problems that came up in the past, and the solutions we used to resolve them:

- The student cannot change his grip on the pencil or continues to grip it too tight. Use or repeat the "baby bird" ploy mentioned earlier: "Remember to hold the pencil just like it was a baby bird. You need to hold it tight enough that it can't get away, but loose enough not to squash it."

- The student asks how to erase the images. Say, "Imagine having an imaginary hand, and in the imaginary hand is a great big eraser. Just reach over with the eraser and erase the pictures."

- The student is surprised at the idea of erasing mental images and asks, "Can I really do that?" Simply say, "Yes, it's easy. Try it and see."

- Sometimes a student will continue to bring up only one picture at a time. After a dozen of so cycles through the process with single pictures, you could drop a hint that more than one can be erased at once.

- The student asks if he can keep a particular picture. Say, "Sure, but you will have to give it a different label. It can't have the label of *what writing should look like*. So give it a new name."

- The student balks at the idea of erasing all of the pictures of *what writing should look like*. Say, "If you want to keep your problem, keep some of the pictures. You don't need any of them. They will just get in the way. You will be replacing them with better ones anyway."

- On rare occasions, a student may not understand that you're only looking for pictures of what writing *should* look like, not pictures of what writing actually *does* look like. This can happen if the student was given the wrong instruction wording or didn't fully understand it. If you have spent more than half an hour repeating the steps with little or no progress, you can ask the student, "Are you erasing pictures of what writing *looks like* or pictures of what writing *should* look like?" Instruct the student that only the *should look like* pictures need to be erased.

CHAPTER 24

Handwriting Correction for Inadequate Natural Orientation

This problem exists apparently because *dyspraxia* has prevented the student's brain from opening the neural pathways for accurate perception. With blocked or distorted perception, the brain cannot accurately instruct the hand to draw the shapes and directions of lines used in handwriting. This procedure will allow you to assist the student in opening new neural pathways—first for accurate perception, and then for creating accurate lines and shapes.

First, a note of caution: You will be pushing your student's tolerance for frustration. You will be asking the student to do something he cannot do, so you must not push too hard, and you must know when to back off.

The assumption is that the student's previous orientation prevented his brain from accessing certain neural pathways. The new orientation you provided will have already removed that block, so the brain is able to access the neural pathways for the first time. The neural pathways must be forced open, a little like unplugging a blocked pipe. But this won't happen until the student forces his brain to do so. He won't be able to do what you ask until the neural pathways are opened.

Perception, Then Coordination

Because there are two sets of neural pathways to be opened, the job is compounded. The pathways for perception will open first. For the first time, the student will be able to perceive the symmetry and shape of a letter accurately. So far, so good.

But he still won't be able to make his hand create the letter. At that point, your student's frustration tolerance level will decrease dramatically. If you allow him to push past his threshold of frustration, he will have what we call an "emotional explosion." We call it that because it's the best description of what happens.

Part of your job is to prevent it from happening. When you see the student's frustration building, you must immediately stop him from doing the activity that is causing it. If you miss the signals and an explosion occurs, stop work for the day. At that point, you may also need to restore the student's motivation before you can begin again. It is best if you don't allow it to occur in the first place. I'll tell you what to watch for and what to do when you see it.

Preparation and Procedure

If you haven't done so already, install the Basic Tools Package outlined in Part II. The student should have a means of controlling disorientation, a method for releasing tension and stress, and a method of controlling his energy level and the speed of his internal clock. The Orientation procedure will allow the student to access the previously blocked neural pathways. To complete the exercise, you will need two pounds of plasteline clay, a plastic knife, and paper towels for cleanup.

PREPARATION

- Set up your workspace.

- Roll out clay cords or "ropes" about ⅜ inch in diameter. Cut them into uniform pieces about three inches long. To begin, you will need at least forty of these pieces. Make more as needed while you work.

- Have the student sit across the table from you.

- Have the student check orientation. For Alignment say, "Feel your imaginary hands on your shoulders." For the Orientation procedure say, "Check your point."

- Have the student do Release.

- Have the student set his Energy Dial to an appropriate setting for this activity.

- Give the student an explanation of what you expect in language appropriate to the student's age. Example: "I am going to ask you to do something you have never done before. Because you have never done it before, it may be difficult and frustrating. I understand that, so we're going to take it slow and easy. We will take a lot of breaks and we will take our time to get through it. Just do what I ask you to do and let it be easy. I'll know it will be the best you can do without working hard at it. It's how often you do it, while letting it be easy, that will get us through it. Every time you try, you will get a little bit better at it."

- Give the student the example to follow:
  Take four pieces of clay and fashion an uppercase letter W. Place it on the middle of the table, facing the student (it will be upside down from your perspective).

PROCEDURE
- Place four pieces of clay the same length as the four lines in your W on the table in front of the student. Point at the example and say, "Take these four pieces of clay and make a letter that looks just like this one." Do not alter the wording; it's appropriate for all ages. An alternate wording could undermine the effectiveness of the procedure. Don't let the student struggle too much. In less than a minute, the student will be pushing

against his threshold of frustration, and you must stop this when it happens. Don't give the student any instructions on how to make the letter look better. The real job being done here is to open neural pathways, not to make a good letter. Once the neural pathways are open, the student won't need your instructions anyway. At this point, any additional instruction would only increase his frustration. If you need to stop the student, reach over and put your hand on the hand he is using to model the clay. Say, "That's good for now." If the student finishes before you need to stop him, simply say, "Good." Immediately remove the student's model and put it aside. Remember, you don't care how it looks.

- Have the student recheck orientation (For Alignment, "Feel your imaginary hands on your shoulders," or for Orientation, "Check your point.") If the student would benefit from doing Release, ask him to do it. If the student would benefit from a change in energy level or sense of time, have him reset his Energy Dial. If the student would benefit from taking a break, take one.

- Repeat the previous instruction step. Put four more pieces of clay in front of the student, and ask the student to "Take these four pieces of clay and make a letter that looks just like this one."

The procedure for opening neural pathways is completed by many repetitions of the instruction step.

In the beginning, the letter the student creates won't look anything like your example. In fact, if it does, you may be barking up the wrong tree—you have probably selected the wrong category of handwriting problem.

It is common to see no improvement whatsoever during many attempts to form the letter *W*. That's because you cannot see where the student is doing the real work: It's happening inside his head. The job will be at least half complete *before* you see any significant improvement in the *W*'s he models on the table. You should watch for any signs of improvement, but don't make any comment if you see them. Improvements signal a change in the student's frustration threshold.

The student's neural pathways for perception will be opened by this process first. Then he will be able to see accurately the example letter he is supposed to copy. This is where you will begin to see improvement. However, the neural pathways for *making* the letter aren't yet opened. When the perception changes, what you might see on the table is one or two straight diagonal lines, or a correct intersection point. This should raise the caution flag.

Warning Signs

From here, you must proceed cautiously. The student's threshold for frustration may have plummeted by as much as 90 percent at this point. Now the difference between what he sees and his attempts to copy it are obvious. If he is allowed to pass his frustration threshold, he will have the emotional explosion described earlier. It's like a bomb with a very short fuse, so you will need to catch it within ten seconds after the fuse is lit. The signs of a lit fuse are usually subtle, but if you are alert they should be obvious. The most common signs are:

- The hands begin to shake or tremble
- Hand and body movements become quick, jerky and erratic
- The body slightly stiffens
- The face will often flush

The moment you notice even one of the signs, act quickly. You don't have the luxury of time to look for supporting evidence. Talking or saying something isn't sufficient. You must physically reach over and grab the student's hand(s) to stop him and break the cycle. Say, "That's fine for now." and take a break. Breaking the cycle puts out the fuse, but it can easily be lit again.

Often the student doesn't want to stop what he is doing. He may think he almost has it, and he's right. But the extreme force he is using to push through the exercise won't get him all the way. You must make him stop! Take a break for at least two minutes before continuing. A ten-minute break and a walk might be even better.

When you come back to this activity, be sure to have the student check Orientation, do Release, and set his

Energy Dial. Before giving the instruction say, "We are getting very close now. So it's especially important that you let it be easy. Just put down one piece of clay at a time. If you want to move them around a little it's okay, but it's better to start over with new pieces than to try and fix it." (Note that there are no negative words in this statement.)

The caution flag is also a signal for a change in your demeanor. Until now you have not praised the student or given any positive reinforcement for his creativity. Now that the goal has shifted to opening the "make it" neural pathways, positive reinforcement will help you move the process along. Remember that in this work, there is no such thing as constructive *criticism*. Leave out all the negatives. To maximize the value of positive reinforcement, it must be specific. Point at a specific item and comment on it positively. It might sound something like this:

"This line is straight, and this line is straight, and this one is almost straight. This (intersecting) point is right, and so is this one. And this angle is almost right. Let's do another one." Then move the student's last attempt aside and lay down four more pieces of clay.

The work usually goes very quickly after this point. Very soon, the student will make a letter that is pretty similar to the model. When this occurs, you could suggest that he place his creation on top of the model to see how accurate it is.

- Repeat the instruction step until complete. This step is complete when the student can create an accurately formed letter *W*. It doesn't have to be perfect, only accurately formed, with straight diagonal lines and points that intersect properly.

At this point, the student's brain can accurately perceive the symmetry of letters and can make straight diagonal lines with appropriate intersections. The reason the student couldn't learn and develop these handwriting skills has been eliminated. The student's perception of the world has doubled in size. A major goal has been attained!

Follow-up Instruction

This is not an end, it is a new beginning. A student with this problem will still be a long way from developing the fine motor skills needed for handwriting in cursive style.

There are many different strategies that would be effective in providing the student the necessary skills for handwriting. Here is the one I feel would be most thorough:

- Repeat the previous procedure using the capital letters *M*, *V*, and *A*. This should go very quickly, although it may take some time before the student sees that two of the lines of the *M* are vertical, not splayed out at an angle as they were for the *W*.

- From Chapter 15, follow the procedures for mastering the upper- and lowercase alphabet.

- Have the student create from clay the cursive alphabet letters in upper- and lowercase.

- Have the student go through the procedures outlined in Chapter 21, "No or Inadequate Instruction."

- At that point, your work with the student will be complete.

GLOSSARY

Acalculia: an inability to develop mathematical skills. *A person with acalculia cannot do arithmetic.*

ADD: acronym and abbreviation for attention deficit disorder. *ADD is described in* The Merck Manual of Diagnosis and Therapy.

Agraphia: an inability to manipulate a writing instrument or express thoughts in writing. *A person with agraphia may speak well but cannot write.*

Alignment procedure: an exercise that can be used as an alternative to Davis Orientation Counseling (described in Chapters 6 and 12).

Alphabet: the letters of a language in their customary order. *The English alphabet has twenty-six letters.*

Arithmetic: determining a quantity by counting or the manipulation of numbers or numerals through addition, subtraction, multiplication, or division. *We learned basic arithmetic in first grade.*

Attention: awareness of the environment. *Attention is what is used when enjoying a beautiful sunset.*

Attention deficit disorder: see ADD.

Auditory: relating to the sense of hearing. *Her auditory talent made it easy to learn singing.*

Balance: ability to stand on one foot without wobbling; a perception that can be used to check orientation. *By checking our balance we can tell if we are oriented.*

Concentration: limiting one's awareness to only one thing. *Heavy concentration produces a hypnotic state.*

Concept: an idea or thought; a mental picture; an idea of what something is, or what a group of things are. *Words are used to communicate a concept.*

Conceptualization: an image, idea, thought, or concept that is created in the mind; the act of mentally creating something. *Conceptualization occurs in the mind.*

Confusion: an overwhelming feeling of blankness. *Confusion causes disorientation in dyslexics.*

Consequence: something happening as the result of something else. *A mistake is often the consequence of disorientation.*

Counseling: helping people improve their abilities or get rid of their disabilities. *We get counseling when we need help with a problem.*

Cursive: written in a flowing style with the letters joined. *After we learned to print, the teacher showed us how to write cursive.*

Davis Orientation Counseling: procedures that help a person create, find, and use a stable location for the mind's eye; methods for controlling, monitoring, and turning off disorientations. *Davis Orientation Counseling shows a person how to self-correct disorientations.*

Davis Orientation Counseling Program: an individualized counseling program where a person learns how to correct disorientations, maintain orientation, and improve reading, writing, math, or attention focus skills. *The Davis Orientation Counseling Program takes about thirty hours to complete.*

Davis Orientation Mastery: the overall name for the diagnostic, therapeutic, and educational procedures developed by Ron Davis. *I trained in the Davis Orientation Mastery procedures.*

Davis Symbol Mastery: a procedure for learning what a symbol means, what it looks like, and what it sounds like. *We create concepts with clay when we do Davis Symbol Mastery.*

Definition: a statement that tells the meaning of a word. *Tell me the definition of that word.*

Disorient: to lose one's position or direction in relation to the true facts and conditions in the environment; to lose touch with reality to some degree. *People who disorient easily sometimes feel dizzy.*

Disorientation: the loss of one's position or direction in relation to other things; a state of mind in which mental perceptions do not agree with the true facts and conditions in the environment; in some people, this is an automatic response to confusion. *During a disorientation the perceptions are altered.*

Dyscalculia: a form of dyslexia where the difficulty is primarily with math and numbers. *A common symptom of dyscalculia is difficulty learning phone numbers.*

Dysgraphia: a form of dyslexia where the difficulty is primarily with handwriting. *People with dysgraphia have problems with penmanship.*

Dyslexia: a type of disorientation caused by a natural cognitive ability that can replace normal sensory perceptions with conceptualizations; reading, writing, speaking, or directional difficulties that stem from disorientations triggered by confusions regarding symbols. *Dyslexia stems from a perceptual talent.*

Dyspraxia: motor difficulties that can affect body motions. *Dyspraxia can manifest as clumsiness, handwriting problems, or speech difficulties.*

Fine-Tuning: the Davis procedure for checking and adjusting orientation using balance (described in Chapter 11). *Fine-Tuning is done three days after an initial Orientation Counseling session.*

Holding: the phenomenon of trying to "hold" the mind's eye in place. *Holding causes headaches.*

Hyperactivity: a condition that can accompany attention deficit disorder where a person appears overly restless, moves about a great deal, and can't sit still. *Hyperactivity is the opposite of lethargy.*

Hypoactivity: a condition that can accompany attention deficit disorder where a person appears less active than normal and performs tasks slowly. The opposite of hyperactivity. *Hypoactivity is often called "laziness."*

Kinesthetic (learning): using the sense of body movement, position, or touch to gain experience. *Playing sports helps develop a student's kinesthetic ability.*

Language: speech sounds that have meaning; written symbols that represent speech sounds; the speech and writing of a particular country or group of people. *The only language I know is English.*

Letter: a written symbol that represents a speech sound. *"Z" is a letter.*

Master: to know with certainty; to practice or do something until it is completely known. *To master something requires practice.*

Mastery: certainty; knowing for sure what something means, looks like, or sounds like; knowing how to do something well; knowing without doubt. *His mastery of cooking makes him an excellent chef.*

Mathematics: determining quantities to study and express relationships between quantities and magnitudes as represented by numbers, numerals, and symbols. *Algebra and calculus are forms of higher mathematics.*

Meaning: an idea someone has attached to an object or symbol. *All words have a meaning.*

Mind's eye: that which views one's mental images. *The mind's eye is what looks at our imagination.*

Motivation: a reason to do something or behave in a certain way. *An interest in how things work was her motivation to study engineering.*

Natural orientation: a general location for the mind's eye that naturally occurs with human development. *A common natural orientation for a gymnast is several feet straight above the head on midline.*

Nonverbal conceptualization: thinking with mental pictures of concepts or ideas; any form of thinking that does not use words. *Intuition is a form of nonverbal conceptualization.*

"Old solutions": see Solutions.

Optimum orientation: placement of the mind's eye that results in all the perceptions being in agreement with each other and accurate; specifically the senses of balance, motion, vision, hearing, and time. *Optimum orientation results from Fine-Tuning.*

Order: Things in their proper places, positions, and conditions. *The dictionary is arranged in alphabetical order.*

Orient: to put oneself in the proper position and state of mind so one's mental perceptions agree with the true facts and conditions in the environment; to position the mind's eye above and behind the head in a stable location. *When we orient ourselves, we can read better.*

Orientation: putting oneself in the proper position in relation to the true facts and conditions; a state of mind in which mental perceptions agree with the true facts and conditions in the environment. *Orientation makes me feel less confused.*

Orientation point: a stable location above and behind the head (this location varies from person to person). *Put your mind's eye on the orientation point.*

Perception: information that comes to the brain through the sensory organs and channels. *We determine what is real with our perception.*

Release: a relaxation and stress relief procedure (described in Chapter 10). *Do Release when you feel tense.*

Responsibility: the ability and willingness to control something. *It's my responsibility to wash the dishes after dinner.*

Review: a procedure used after Orientation Counseling to check if the orientation point is located in the proper place. *Do Review with the student at least once a day until fine-tuning is complete.*

Sequence: How things follow each other, one after another. *Our numerical system follows a certain sequence.*

Solutions (compulsive): behaviors, habits, and mental tricks adopted to resolve the mistakes and frustrations caused by disorientation; the components of a learning disability. *Having to sing the Alphabet Song is a common solution to not being able to learn the alphabet.*

Stable orientation: a condition in which a person's mind's eye tends to remain in one location most or all of the time. *People who do not experience dyslexic symptoms tend to have a stable orientation.*

Symbol: something that means or represents something else. *The flag is a symbol of our country.*

Threshold for confusion: the point at which the confusion in the environment becomes overwhelming to an individual. *When dyslexics reach their threshold for confusion, they become disoriented.*

Time: the measurement of change according to a standard. *One hour of time is equal to ¹/₂₄ of the earth's rotation on its axis, a worldwide standard.*

Trigger (word): anything that causes disorientation; usually a word or symbol for which a person does not have a complete or accurate concept. *The word "the" is a common trigger word.*

Unstable orientation: a condition in which a person's mind's eye moves about a lot. *People who experience motion sickness easily tend to have an unstable orientation.*

Verbal conceptualization: thinking with the sounds of words. *Hearing your thoughts in words is a form of verbal conceptualization.*

Word: a spoken sound, or letters that represent that sound, which have a meaning or definition in a language. *I learned a new word today.*

RECOMMENDED BOOKS

ADD/ADHD

Attention Deficit Disorder: A Different Perception, Thom Hartmann.
Provides many good reasons for "distractable" people to celebrate their ability to perceive multi-dimensionally. Highly recommended for anyone interested in understanding Attention Deficit Disorder.

The Myth of the ADD Child: 50 Ways to Improve Your Child's Behavior and Attention Span Without Drugs, Labels or Coercion, Thomas Armstrong, Ph.D.
A must-have book for any parent whose child fits the ADD profile. If anyone has suggested medication for your child, read this before making a decision!

Right-Brained Children in a Left-Brained World: Unlocking the Potential of Your ADD Child, Jeffrey Freed & Laurie Parsons.
Explores a variety of innovative and sometimes surprising approaches to teaching the ADD Child.

HANDWRITING AND COMPOSITION

Checking Your Grammar, Scholastic Guides.
Helps students find answers to grammar questions quickly, includes spelling, punctuation, capitalization, contractions, parts of speech, abbreviations, acronyms, and the 100 most often confused and misused words.

Cursive Connections Workbook, Kathryn Libby.
Over seventy reproducible pages for developing cursive writing skills.

Putting it in Writing, Scholastic Guides.
Provides young writers with models written by real kids, organized by types of letters and school reports. Filled with tips and examples.

MATH

Barron's Mathematics Study Dictionary, Frank Tapson.
An indispensible reference for intermediate to advanced math students. Comprehensive definitions and explanations of mathematical terms, organized by concept.

Exploring Time, Gillian Chapman & Pam Robson.
Projects suitable for ages 5–9 that teach the basic concept of time as measurement.

Math-a-pedia: Primary, Addison-Wesley Publishing.
Presents the basic vocabulary of arithmetic and math for children ages 5–8.

Math-a-pedia: Intermediate, Addison-Wesley Publishing.
Illustrates basic math concepts including fractions, factors, and
statistics for ages 8–14.

*Yes You Can! Help Your Kid Succeed in Math Even if You
Think You Can't,* Jean Bullard and Louise Osborne.
Advice for parents and strategies for overcoming math anxiety
and other barriers to learning. A great resource for those who
don't know where to start.

THE CREATIVE MIND

In the Mind's Eye, Thomas G. West.
An in-depth look at the connections between creative ability,
visual thinking, and academic learning difficulties. Explores the
minds of famous dyslexics from Einstein to Churchill.

Strong-Willed Child or Dreamer?, Dana Spears & Ron Braund.
A must for parents of children who are imaginative, sensitive,
moody, stubborn, and compassionate.

*Uniquely Gifted: Identifying and Meeting the Needs of the
Twice-Exceptional Student,* ed. Kiesa Kay.
An anthology of articles geared to the exceptional needs of
students who are both intellectually gifted and struggle with
learning differences.

Upside-Down Brilliance: The Visual-Spatial Learner, Linda
Kreger Silverman, Ph.D.
Explores learning needs and educational strategies, supported by
research studies that indicate 37 percent of students are visual-
spatial learners.

Your Child's Growing Mind: A Practical Guide to Brain Development and Learning from Birth to Adolescence, Jane Healy, Ph.D.
An essential guide to how children learn, with specific suggestions on ways to direct each child toward academic success.

DICTIONARIES

The Concise Oxford Dictionary of Current English Although you might need a magnifying glass, when it comes to the Queen's English, there is no better reference. This is where you will find literary or obscure definitions for a word.

The Macmillan Visual Dictionary A full color dictionary covering 600 subjects. Identifies over 25,000 terms with detailed, accurate illustrations. A picture thinker's dream come true.

Webster's New World Children's Dictionary Clearly written, well formatted and nicely illustrated, this dictionary is excellent for doing Symbol Mastery with all age groups.

INDEX

The Davis Symbol Mastery Kit

A wealth of materials to teach basic literacy skills "through their fingers." Homeschooling parents, teachers and educational therapists around the world are using this method successfully.

Symbol Mastery isn't just for dyslexics. This kit helps any child learn the alphabet, basic writing symbols and the small words in a way that's fun and easy. Teenage and adult dyslexics can use it to improve their reading, writing, and spelling. Includes:

- Instruction manual with checklist
- Symbol Mastery Steps video (155 min.)
- Symbol Mastery Steps poster
- Upper- and lowercase alphabet strip, used for Alphabet Mastery
- Letter recognition cards with large letters, specially designed for younger children
- Stop Signs in Reading punctuation poster
- Punctuation Marks and Style booklet
- Pronunciation Key cards
- Our favorite dictionary and grammar book
- Two pounds of artist's modeling clay

. . . all in a sturdy bag with shoulder strap.

Davis Symbol Mastery Kit

Davis Orientation Videos

The Assessment and Orientation procedures described in *The Gift of Learning* presented in how-to form. Just follow the steps as demonstrated by Ron Davis.

The worldwide best-selling book about learning disability, now on audio CD

Read by the author
4 Compact Discs
Total listening time:
4 hours, 28 minutes

The Dyslexic Reader Newsletter

A quarterly publication with articles on the dyslexic learning style, plus tips on applying the Davis procedures. Ask for a FREE copy!

The Gift of Dyslexia audiobook

Ron Davis' ground-breaking first book, read by the author on audiotape or CD.

Join Davis Dyslexia Association International (DDAI) and deduct 10% from your order! Membership includes newsletter subscription and supports worldwide information services.

▶ ORDER FORM ▶

O·R·D·E·R   F·O·R·M

Quant.	Item	Price	Total
_____	_The Gift of Dyslexia_ (paperback)	$14.95	$_____
_____	Extra copies of _The Gift of Learning_ (paperback)	$14.95	$_____
_____	_The Gift of Dyslexia_ on audiotape	$29.95	$_____
_____	_The Gift of Dyslexia_ on CD	$39.95	$_____
_____	Symbol Mastery Kit	$139.95	$_____
_____	Assessment & Orientation Video set	$64.95	$_____
_____	_The Dyslexic Reader_ Newsletter - sample issue		$ FREE
_____	Professional Training Information		$ FREE
_____	Davis Dyslexia Correction Program Information		$ FREE
	Subtotal for shipping charges		$_____
	Deduct 10% if joining Davis Dyslexia Association		$_____
	Calif. residents: add sales tax (.0825 x subtotal)		$_____
	Shipping (see chart below)		$_____
_____	DDAI Membership: ☐ $50*/yr. ☐ $80*/2 yrs.		$_____
_____	Newsletter subscription only: ☐ $25*/yr. ☐ $40*/2 yrs.		$_____
	*Add $5/yr for Canada/Mexico; $10/yr. other countries		$_____
	GRAND TOTAL		$_____

U.S. Shipping Rates

Subtotal amnt. (from above)	Book rate	First Class	Note: Foreign orders must use a credit card.
Up to $20.00	$4.50	Add $2.00 for First Class; add $3.00 for Canada and Mexico	Outside North America, airmail or fax this form to +1 (650) 692-7075. We'll add airmail postage plus $5.00 for handling.
$20.01-$40.00	$6.50		
$40.01-$60.00	$8.00		
Over $60.01	$10.00		

Credit card: ☐ Visa   ☐ MasterCard   ☐ Discover   ☐ American Express

Card number: _____ _____ _____ _____   Expiration date: _____

Name on card: _____

Signature: _____   Phone: (____) _____

Ship to: _____

Street address: _____

City/State: _____   Zip code: _____

To order by mail or fax:

Send this page with check or credit card information to:

Davis Dyslexia Association International
1601 Old Bayshore Highway, Suite 245
Burlingame, CA 94010

Or fax to +1 (650) 692-7075

To order by phone:

Call toll-free: 1-888-999-3324 or 1-650-692-7141

You can also contact us and order materials through our Internet site:

http://www.dyslexia.com or via e-mail: **gift@dyslexia.com**